TIMEFORM

C000003248

HORSES TO FOLLOW

2023 FLAT SEASON

CONTENTS

TIMEF⬤RM

ISBN 978-1-8380349-5-5 Price £10.95

Printed and bound by
Charlesworth Press,
Wakefield, UK 01924 204830

SECTION

Timeform's Fifty To Follow, carefully chosen by members of Timeform's editorial staff, are listed below with their respective page numbers. A selection of ten (**marked in bold with a ★**) is made for those who prefer a smaller list.

The form summary for each horse is shown after its age, colour, sex and pedigree. The summary shows the distance, the state of the going and where the horse finished in each of its races on the Flat during 2022. Performances are in chronological sequence with the date of its last race shown at the end.

The distance of each race is given in furlongs, fractional distances being expressed in the decimal notation to the nearest tenth of a furlong. Races run in Britain on all-weather surfaces are prefixed by 'f' for fibresand, 'p' for polytrack and 't' for tapeta.

The going is symbolised as follows: f=firm (turf) or fast (all-weather), m=good to firm (turf) or standard to fast (all-weather); g=good (turf) or standard (all-weather), d=good to soft/dead (turf) or standard to slow (all-weather); s=soft (turf) or slow (all-weather); v=heavy.

Placings are indicated, up to the sixth place, by use of superior figures, an asterisk being used to denote a win.

The Timeform Rating of a horse is simply the merit of the horse expressed in pounds and is arrived at by careful examination of its running against other horses. The ratings range from 130+ for tip-top performers down to a figure of around 20 for the poorest. Symbols attached to the ratings: 'p'–likely to improve; 'P'–capable of much better form; '+'–the horse may be better than we have rated it.

Aimeric 103

4 b.g. Frankel – Aris (Ire) (Danroad (Aus))
2022 10.2m² 10g⁴ 12.3g* 13.9m 13.1g* 13.9d Oct 7

Aimeric was twice a winner during his debut campaign in 2022 despite leaving the overall impression that the penny hadn't quite dropped with him, still looking a bit rough around the edges and very much the type to go on to better things as a four-year-old.

A well-backed 15/8 favourite when making his debut in a Nottingham maiden in April, Aimeric shaped with plenty of promise in filling the runner-up spot, doing well to be beaten just a length and three-quarters having started his run from a good bit further back than the winner, Savvy Knight. That rival advertised the strength of that form when winning his next two starts—running to a useful level in the process—and Aimeric wasn't long in opening his account as he bounced back from an underwhelming effort at Newmarket in between to win a small-field maiden at Chester in July, clearly relishing the step up to a mile and a half as he stayed on well to land the spoils by half a length.

Aimeric was then thrown in at the deep end for the Sky Bet Melrose at York's Ebor Festival in August and shaped better than the bare result on handicap debut, ultimately finishing in mid-division having looked threatening for a long way. However, it was when he won a warm-looking contest over 13 furlongs at Ayr next time that he really marked himself out as a promising stayer, finishing strongly to lead in the final strides. The official winning margin was just a short head, but he was arguably value for extra having come from further back than anything else in the frame, showing useful form and yet still looking far from the finished article (hung left entering the final furlong).

On his final three-year-old start Aimeric was well held at York, but he seemed unsuited by the conditions (on softer ground than previously) and is better judged on the form he showed at Ayr. Gelded during the winter, he starts his four-year-old campaign on a BHA mark of 92 and all the high-end staying handicaps are likely to be on his agenda. Yet to race beyond a mile and three-quarters, he seems sure to have more to offer as his stamina is drawn out further. **Roger Varian**

Conclusion: *Unexposed stayer who was raw as a three-year-old and should come into his own faced with stiffer tests this year (likely to stay 2m)*

 # Al Husn (Ire) 108p

4 b.f. Dubawi (Ire) – Hadaatha (Ire) (Sea The Stars (Ire))
2022 p8s* 8m* 10g* Oct 1

Roger Varian has a most progressive filly for Shadwell on his hands in Al Husn, who looks destined to make an impact in Group company as a four-year-old. She hasn't had much racing, with just three starts in the autumn of her two-year-old season and another three outings last year, but she's now won her last four starts. She got off the mark late in 2021 in a novice at Kempton despite still not looking the finished article, flashing her tail and edging right but creating a positive impression overall as she was well on top at the finish. Al Husn then returned over the same course and distance last April when taking on five other winning fillies in a conditions race, looking much more polished there as she showed a good turn of foot at the end of a steadily-run race to win readily by a length from Golden Mayflower.

Further progress from Al Husn looked likely but it was to be another five months before she got the chance to prove it when making her handicap debut at Newmarket in September. That proved a red-letter day for her stable as Al Husn was one of no fewer than seven winners from 12 runners for her yard spread over three meetings, with Sakheer's win in the Mill Reef Stakes at Newbury being the highlight. Al Husn was back on turf for the first time since her debut a year earlier and resumed from her break with another improved effort. Travelling strongly, Al Husn loomed into contention and kept on to beat Eidikos by a length and a quarter once Dane O'Neill produced her to lead over a furlong out.

Two weeks later, Al Husn was stepped up to a mile and a quarter for the first time for a more valuable fillies' contest where her rivals included four other last-time-out

Al Husn (right) looks a pattern performer in the making

winners. Clearly still improving in leaps and bounds, Al Husn completed her four-timer by half a length and looked value for a bit extra as she had to weave a passage through a tightly-packed field to hit the front inside the final furlong. That proved very strong form with four of the beaten fillies successful next time. The second and third, Something Enticing and Bellstreet Bridie, won a listed race and a US Grade 3 contest, respectively, which is the sort of company Al Husn should be competitive in herself before long. **Roger Varian**

Conclusion: *Lightly-raced and most progressive filly who completed a four-timer in a high-quality fillies' handicap at Newmarket on her final three-year-old start; well worth her place in better company this term*

Al Nafir (Ire) 107p

4 ch.g. Dubawi (Ire) – Nightime (Ire) (Galileo (Ire))
2022 10m² 13.9m⁵ 12g⁶ 12g* Oct 7

Al Nafir is bred in the purple and has the looks to match but, in truth, for much of his fledgling career he'll have been viewed as a costly flop by the big-spending Godolphin operation. Indeed, the decision to shell out €1,200,000 on this imposing chestnut as a foal had yielded just one win—in a £3,780 Kempton novice on his final outing at two—from five starts by the time he lined up for the Old Rowley Cup over a mile and a half at Newmarket in October, where he was sent off the 16/1 seventh choice in a competitive field of 16. His convincing victory off a BHA mark of 90 at Newmarket changed all of that, though. While swelling those prize money coffers to the tune of a further £61,848, the more significant dividend was that Al Nafir took his form to new levels that day with the promise of further improvement still.

In truth, Al Nafir had hinted at a bigger performance several times before (notably when a non-staying fifth in the Sky Bet Melrose at York), while even his neck defeat of stable-companion Wild Crusade at Newmarket rather undersells him as he always had matters under control after edging ahead a furlong out. His pedigree screams that there should be better to come, too. His dam Nightime won the 2006 Irish 1000 Guineas, while he's a full-brother to the top-class Ghaiyyath, who was a multiple Group 1 winner in the same silks for Charlie Appleby. In addition, their half-sister Zhukova (by Fastnet Rock) was a very smart prolific winner who, like Ghaiyyath, seemed best at up to a mile and a half. That appeals as the optimum trip for the now-gelded Al Nafir, though he'd have no issue coping with a well-run race over a mile and a quarter. He seems sure to pay his way in valuable handicaps and/or pattern company in 2023. *Charlie Appleby*

Conclusion: *Finally put it all together when signing off last season with a comfortable victory in the Old Rowley Cup at Newmarket; pedigree and physique both point to him making further progress as a four-year-old*

Animate (Ire) 90

3 b.g. Shamardal (USA) – Dark Liberty (Ire) (Dark Angel (Ire))
2022 7g⁴ p7s³ t7.1s* 8g⁴ Sep 17

Dark Liberty was a progressive filly and, despite racing only as a two-year-old, showed useful form when successful in listed company on her final start. Her second foal, Animate, couldn't quite match that level as a juvenile in four starts for the same connections, winning one of them, but there are plenty of reasons to think he can better it as a three-year-old.

Having made the frame in a pair of novice events on his first two runs, both won by Charlie Appleby inmates, namely Victory Dance and Silver Knott, Animate then showed much improved form when making all in a similar event at Newcastle, finding plenty and pulling clear of the rest with a next-time-out winner. As a result, Animate looked well-in for his nursery debut when stepped up to a mile at Ayr and, although he was unable to justify 6/4 favouritism, he still shaped well as he passed the post around three lengths behind the winner in fourth. He found some trouble and was also a bit too keen on his first try at the trip, holding every chance a furlong out before his early exertions seemed to take their toll.

The Ayr form looks strong—Animate split a pair of subsequent winners—and there's no doubt that he'll prove himself fully effective over a mile in time. Gelded during the winter, he is certainly in the right hands to improve with age and will surely prove his mark lenient in the short term, with the potential there for him to progress through the ranks. **Simon & Ed Crisford**

Conclusion: *Still unexposed and his Ayr run suggests he's on a workable mark with a view to three-year-old handicaps at around 1m*

Arkendale   88p

3 br.c. Pivotal – Paris Rooftops (Ire) (Galileo (Ire))
2022 8g^2 8d^4 Oct 17

Arkendale shaped with distinct promise in both his runs as a two-year-old, starting out with an eye-catching effort behind Salt Bay at Haydock on his debut in September before finding a listed contest at Pontefract too hot on his only other outing in October. The overall impression he created was that of a horse with whom connections had barely scratched the surface and it could be that another winter on his back will be the making of him.

That Haydock debut form has been franked handsomely since, the winner subsequently placed in Group 1 company in France, and Arkendale left the impression he'd have given Salt Bay more to think about had things gone more his way, never nearer having been forced to weave his way through. The fact he was then pitched into listed company is presumably indicative of the regard in which he's held and, while he lacked the required nous to get seriously involved from the worst of the draw, it should have aided his development plenty.

Arkendale should have no problem picking up a novice or maiden, after which he'll have a mark, and that's where Ed Walker's typically patient approach has paid dividends with similar types. There should be opportunities aplenty for him this season with no shortage of valuable three-year-old handicaps in the racing calendar, and he can pay his way over the course of 2023. **Ed Walker**

Conclusion: *Offered encouragement in both starts at two and appeals as the type to progress well and make an impact in high-end three-year-old handicaps at around 1m*

Astral Beau 95

4 b.f. Brazen Beau (Aus) – Asteroidea (Sea The Stars (Ire))
2022 7s* 7g⁴ 7m⁴ 8g³ 8.2m 7d* 7m* 7d² 7s* Oct 29

For an operation that only ever has a handful of horses across both codes, Pam Sly's Cambridgeshire yard has long been one that punches above its weight, something that was never more evident than when Speciosa won the 1,000 Guineas back in 2006. Sly has trained plenty of Speciosa's descendants in the 17 years since that famous day at Newmarket, and none has proved anything like as good as their illustrious predecessor, though the filly Astral Beau—who is out of Speciosa's daughter Asteroidea—made up into a useful performer in her first season racing in 2022 and should progress further this year, with a graduation to black-type level not out of the question.

It's no surprise that Astral Beau was a 50/1 shot for her debut at Leicester in April, considering the stable had sent out just one previous winning debutant on the Flat, a

Astral Beau won four times in a productive three-year-old campaign

feat not even Speciosa managed, but she belied those odds to run out an authoritative winner over a host of fairly useful rivals. The progress that effort promised wasn't immediately forthcoming as she was beaten on her next four outings, including in a couple of handicaps, but Astral Beau was well and truly back on the up by the end of the summer and into the autumn. First-time cheekpieces did the trick when she was a narrow winner on the July course at the end of August, and a 2 lb rise for that wasn't enough to stop her following up in a better race on the Rowley Mile three weeks later. She improved again when second, pulling clear with a next-time winner, in a big field at York on her penultimate outing, and shrugged off another small rise when beating 16 rivals back at Newmarket on her final start, proving on that occasion that she doesn't need headgear to produce her best.

Astral Beau's habit of not winning by too far has helped keep her ahead of the handicapper, and hopefully that trend can continue in 2023, when she'll resume from a BHA mark of 86 that will enable her to tackle some more valuable handicaps. She's versatile as regards ground, having won on both soft and good to firm, and seems suited by a galloping track. *Pam Sly*

Conclusion: *Progressed well through a three-year-old season that yielded four wins and looks the type to raise her game further this year, potentially even graduating beyond handicaps*

 # Awaal (Ire)   114p

4 b.g. Lope de Vega (Ire) – Anna's Rock (Ire) (Rock of Gibraltar (Ire))
2022 t7.2d³ p8g* 8m² 8s* Oct 24

Breton Rock was a smart performer as a three-year-old and progressed from handicaps into pattern company the following year, a career trajectory which bodes well for the future of his half-brother, Awaal. Trained by Simon and Ed Crisford, who collected over £1 million in prize money in 2022, he was successful on two of his four starts as a three-year-old, improving with every outing, and is an exciting prospect for the season ahead.

Awaal boasted some strong form in novice events in the spring, first shaping with plenty of promise when third on his debut at Wolverhampton in April—the pair who beat him both had the benefit of previous experience and went on to show useful form—and then narrowly defeating the subsequent Britannia winner Thesis at Lingfield two weeks later, showing a good attitude to get the verdict by a short head as the first two pulled clear of the rest. Awaal progressed further despite meeting with defeat in another novice event at Haydock next time, ultimately passing the post three quarters of a length behind Phantom Flight, who ended the campaign with a Timeform rating of 116. However, it was five months later, when making his handicap debut at

Redcar, that Awaal really left a lasting impression. Sent off the 15/8 favourite, he made a mockery of his opening BHA mark of 93, leading on the bridle inside the final two furlongs before forging clear to record an emphatic three-and-three-quarter-length success from some battled-hardened northern handicappers.

Gelded during the winter, Awaal still looks one step ahead of the handicapper from a 9 lb higher mark and everything about him suggests he'll be suited by the top-end handicaps at around a mile, with a race such as the Hunt Cup at Royal Ascot appealing as a suitable target. A step up in grade will surely await beyond that and his yard showed what they could do with a similar type last season in the shape of Jadoomi, who was last seen finishing third in the Queen Elizabeth II Stakes at Ascot having started the campaign with a lower Timeform rating than Awaal currently has. **Simon & Ed Crisford**

Conclusion: *Unexposed sort who can continue to progress through the handicap ranks before stepping up in grade later in the season*

Patrick Jupp (Awaal): *"For the second year running—following Mujtaba in 2022—I'm putting up an impressive winner of a backend Redcar handicap as my one to watch, in the shape of lightly-raced Awaal. The Redcar event was essentially ordinary, but Awaal still made a mockery of his opening mark and his form from earlier that year looks very solid. On his second outing he beat future Britannia winner Thesis off level weights and he then made the now-smart Phantom Flight work hard at Haydock. A gelding operation over the winter looks no bad thing for this enthusiastic type and, with more progress in the pipeline after just four starts, he looks sure to be of interest in top-end handicaps."*

Caph Star 101p

4 b.c. Siyouni (Fr) – Caskelena (Ire) (Galileo (Ire))
2022 8g³ p8s* Aug 3

Kazakhstan-born owner Nurlan Bizakov enjoyed a purple patch in France at the beginning of October when three of his two-year-old colts won valuable contests in the space of a week. Belbek provided the owner with a first Group 1 win in his pale blue and yellow silks—the colours of the Kazakhstan flag—when winning the Prix Jean-Luc Lagardere at Longchamp a day after Souzak won a valuable sales race at the same track. The following weekend it was the turn of Charyn to win the Group 2 Criterium de Maisons-Laffitte at Chantilly. Charyn is trained by Roger Varian, who has previously trained the Group 3-winning fillies Altyn Orda, Tomyris and Nausha for Bizakov, and connections look to have another good prospect on their hands with the four-year-old colt Caph Star.

Unraced at two, Caph Star didn't make his debut until last July when sent off even-money for a novice at Ffos Las. Although unsuccessful, he shaped with promise after a slow start and kept on in the final furlong after getting outpaced to finish third behind a pair who have shown useful form since, Postmark and Al Agaila. The following month, Caph Star was well backed for a similar event at Kempton and this time justified favouritism, impressing with a burst of acceleration which quickly put the race to bed. Again slowly away, Caph Star quickened to lead over a furlong out and won readily by two and a quarter lengths from Baltimore Boy. The runner-up in turn finished clear of the rest and both the first two showed improved form, Caph Star putting up a useful performance which promised plenty for the remainder of the season, but he wasn't seen out again.

Caph Star's two races at three were over a mile, but he's bred to be at least as effective over longer trips. He's a half-brother to two winners, including Casima, who was a winner at up to a mile and a half despite being by sprinter Dark Angel, while his lightly-raced dam, Caskelena, was a winner at a mile and a quarter in the Bizakov colours for Sir Michael Stoute. She was also a sister to Ballydoyle's high-class stayer Age of Aquarius, who was beaten just a neck in the Gold Cup. **Roger Varian**

Conclusion: *Won the second of his two starts last year with an impressive turn of foot, showing useful form, and has scope for plenty more improvement over 1m+*

Chesspiece   92p
3 b.c. Nathaniel (Ire) – Royal Solitaire (Ire) (Shamardal (USA))
2022 t10.2s* Nov 11

A two-year-old by Nathaniel making a winning debut at Newcastle in November has good portents. It was back in 2016 that a filly named Enable did just that and her subsequent record-breaking achievements scarcely need spelling out. Things would have to go extremely well for Chesspiece to prove anything like that good, but there was certainly an awful lot of promise evident in his own first-time-out win, and he looks a three-year-old to keep on the right side in 2023.

Nathaniel isn't the only middle-distance influence in Chesspiece's pedigree, as his dam was smart at up to a mile and a quarter in Germany and most others in the family have proved best over at least that far. It's no surprise, therefore, that Chesspiece started out over the same trip in a maiden that looked a hot race on paper with several big yards represented. Significantly, Chesspiece was the shortest-priced of the debutants at 100/30 and he justified that market confidence in good style, quickening up well and showing a nice attitude when tackled in the final furlong to land the spoils by a length. Well-bred newcomers from the Johnston and Gosden stables completed the frame to give the form a really solid look and the runner-up, Hadrianus, duly went one better on his next start at Kempton the following month. Developing into a top-end handicapper will probably be the very least of the Crisfords' expectations for Chesspiece this season and there's no doubt at all that he'll be suited by at least a mile and a half. **Simon & Ed Crisford**

Conclusion: *Smartly-bred sort who created a fine impression when winning a hot-looking race on debut and promises to thrive over 1½m+ as a three-year-old*

Chillingham (Ire) 101p

4 b.g. Ulysses (Ire) – Last Jewel (Ire) (Invincible Spirit (Ire))
2022 10g⁵ 10g* t11.1g³ 12v* Sep 3

Chillingham only made his debut in June of his three-year-old campaign and, by the time he signed off for the season less than three months later, he'd made up into a useful performer, winning two of his four starts along the way. He'll do well to sustain such rapid progress again in 2023, but that's not to say he's reached anything like his limit yet and he strikes as just the type to make his mark in some of the more valuable middle-distance handicaps for the up-and-coming Ed Bethell yard.

Chillingham was an eyecatcher when fifth on his debut over a mile and a quarter in what proved a hot novice by Redcar standards, and he was quick to confirm that promise just under three weeks later when doing well to score from off the pace over the same trip at Pontefract. A steady gallop worked against him at Southwell next time, but he still advanced his form in third, conceding both race position and weight to the pair who beat him. Chillingham then went to Thirsk for his handicap debut and an opening mark of 84 proved wholly inadequate as he once again powered through from the rear to lead two furlongs out and drew right away for a three-length win, finishing with an impressive flourish on his first go over a mile and a half considering the heavy ground.

A subsequent 6 lb rise leaves Chillingham still well treated on the bare form he achieved that day, and that's without considering the potential he has for more progress after just four starts. He is something of a free-goer who has worn a hood so far, though that hasn't stopped him proving strong at the finish every time and there's enough stamina in his pedigree to think he'll stay beyond a mile and a half. There's probably no rush to get him up in trip, though, and perhaps one of the middle-distance handicaps at the Dante Festival will prove an ideal early-season target. Wherever he does reappear, he's sure to be one of the least exposed and most progressive types in the line-up. He is effective on tapeta and heavy ground but is yet to encounter going firmer than good. **Edward Bethell**

Conclusion: *Showed rapid improvement in four quick runs as a three-year-old and a similar trajectory should see him go on and make his mark in high-end middle-distance handicaps*

Chorlton Lane (Ire) 86p

3 b.g. Mehmas (Ire) – Asmeen (Ire) (Shamardal (USA))
2022 t7.1s* :: 2023 p7s² Jan 7

After seven seasons of racing, 2022 was the first year that Charlie Fellowes was without his stable star Prince of Arran, who was best known for his exploits in Australia where he was placed in three consecutive runnings of the Melbourne Cup. Prince of Arran may have been retired, but Fellowes had the biggest win of his training career so far last year when two-year-old Marbaan landed the Group 2 Vintage Stakes at Goodwood. Stablemate Chorlton Lane might not be destined to reach the same heights himself, but he appeals as the type to win races as a three-year-old.

Fellowes sent Chorlton Lane to Newcastle for his debut in September where his task was made easier when the strong favourite Oh So Charming had to be withdrawn after becoming upset in the stalls. That left Chorlton Lane with seven rivals to beat, all bar the rank outsider fellow newcomers, and he accomplished his task at the end of a slowly-run race without having to come off the bridle. Produced by Jamie Spencer to lead over a furlong out, Chorlton Lane was clear when edging to his left inside the final furlong and came home with three and three-quarter lengths to spare over The King's Men. It turned out that Chorlton Lane didn't beat much of consequence there, but he confirmed himself a promising sort when contesting a novice at Kempton on his next start in early-January. Taking a strong hold, he led on the bridle over two furlongs out but was worn down close home by the Juddmonte filly Floating Spirit who was making her debut. There was no disgrace in that defeat, as Chorlton Lane was conceding almost a stone to a potentially useful type who landed the odds with plenty in hand on her next start.

Picked up for 27,000 guineas as a yearling, Chorlton Lane looks like proving well bought. There's a mix of speed and stamina in his pedigree as he's by smart sprinter Mehmas, who didn't race beyond the age of two, and from a good Aga Khan family on his dam's side. His dam never made it to the racecourse but was out of a Sadler's Wells half-sister to the top-class middle-distance performer Azamour, whose wins included the King George VI and Queen Elizabeth Stakes and Irish Champion Stakes. *Charlie Fellowes*

Conclusion: *Has impressed with the way he's gone about things in his two starts on the all-weather and looks the type to improve further for having more cover in handicaps*

Follow us on Twitter @Timeform

Coppice 96P

3 b.f. Kingman – Helleborine (Observatory (USA))
2022 p7s* Oct 19

Few juveniles create such a big impression in such a short amount of time as Calyx, who in the space of 10 days in 2018 spreadeagled a strong Newmarket maiden and then overcame a draw bias in the Coventry Stakes, looking "a colt right out of the top drawer" according to our reporter at Royal Ascot. Sadly, injuries prevented him from fulfilling his huge potential—he ran just twice more as a three-year-old—but John Gosden may now feel like he's got a second bite of the cherry with this family courtesy of Coppice, a sister to Calyx.

Although unable to match Calyx and achieve a Timeform rating in the 100s on debut, it's hard not to draw parallels between Coppice and her sibling given the impression she created on her sole two-year-old start, earning a high figure when justifying odds-on favouritism in a seven-furlong novice at Kempton in October. She was produced to lead inside the final furlong having travelled fluently and quickly asserted from there to win by a length and three-quarters with a bit in hand. There was substance to go with the style of that debut success, too, given that the one she pulled clear with, Whispering Dream, won next time and is very much a useful prospect in his own right. A timefigure of 77 coupled with a hefty sectional uplift also fully justifies a Timeform rating of 96P for Coppice, who has the large 'P' to denote that she is open to significant improvement.

Calyx was more about speed than stamina and raced only at six furlongs, but Coppice has already shown herself a slightly different type and both her strength at the finish at Kempton and her pedigree point to her being suited by a mile as a three-year-old. She looks just the type to make up into a pattern performer in 2023 and will be one to watch out for in a 1000 Guineas trial. *John & Thady Gosden*

Conclusion: *Hails from a talented family and looked an exciting prospect when winning her sole start as a juvenile in the style of a pattern-race performer*

Courage Mon Ami 103P

4 b.g. Frankel – Crimson Ribbon (USA) (Lemon Drop Kid (USA))
2022 p12s* t12.4s* Oct 24

"Courage, mon ami, le diable est mort" or, in English, "courage my friend, the devil is dead" is a favoured retort of one of the characters in Charles Reade's 1861 novel The Cloister And The Hearth, a novel described by Sir Arthur Conan in an 1898 article as "the wisest and the most beautiful I have ever read". In that article, Doyle refers to Reade's wonderful reproduction of "that atmosphere of wonder and of adventure which pervaded the world" at a time when the land "over the river, or beyond the mountains" was "all a land of mystery".

Given that the list of very talented horses who have made their debut on the all-weather for John Gosden (with or without his son Thady on the licence) is a significant one, featuring classic winners such as Enable and Jack Hobbs, this season hopefully won't prove "a land of mystery" for Courage Mon Ami, the highly-promising son of Frankel set to step out of the relatively calm waters of all-weather novice races.

Courage Mon Ami was strong in the betting and immediately looked a smart prospect when making a successful debut at Kempton in November, storming clear late on to land the spoils by five lengths. To win by such a wide margin was particularly impressive given that he looked desperately in need of the experience early on (very slowly away and ran green), leaving him with plenty to do to reel in the favourite entering the final two furlongs. Sent off at very prohibitive odds on his next outing at Newcastle in October, he didn't need to do any more in pure form terms to maintain his unbeaten start, but there was again plenty to like about the style of his performance, picking up well in a steadily-run race to win by six lengths with plenty to spare.

Courage Mon Ami, who has been gelded since that Newcastle win, is closely related to Crimson Rosette—a listed winner for Charlie Fellowes who ended her career with a close third in a Group 3—and Purple Ribbon, also trained by Fellowes, who was a very close second in a listed race at Kempton in November. Courage Mon Ami's connections must harbour aspirations that he can go at least that high, with every chance that he'll stay further than a mile and a half. **John & Thady Gosden**

Conclusion: *Created an excellent impression in winning both starts on the all-weather in the autumn; in excellent hands and remains open to significant improvement*

Coverdale (Ire)   79p

3 b.g. Expert Eye – Brynica (Fr) (Desert Style (Ire))
2022 7g 7.8m⁴ 7m³ 8d² Oct 17

Coverdale might have failed to win in 2022, but his four-race juvenile campaign looks to have laid the ideal foundations for future success. Having been held back by inexperience on his first two starts, he showed he was beginning to get the hang of things on his final qualifying run at Redcar in September, sticking on over seven furlongs in the style of one sure to be suited by further. Stepped up to a mile for his nursery debut at Pontefract in October, he duly took a significant step forward and should probably have won all things being equal, doing well to pass the post just a neck behind the similarly improved winner having conceded first run to that rival entering the straight.

Coverdale was clearly well suited by the stiff mile at Pontefract and the way he shaped there suggests he'll stay further than that, especially with another winter on his back. There should certainly be more to come from him having been gelded since his Pontefract run and he's in the right hands to carry on progressing. It's well worth nothing that Ed Bethell, who has enjoyed a couple of very solid years since taking over from his father James, was able to eke out gradual improvement from several of the three-year-olds in his care last season, including Sandbeck, fellow *Fifty* member Chillingham and Reel Rosie. The last named improved markedly for longer trips and had left her opening BHA mark of 71 well behind by the end of the year, something which Coverdale looks well placed to emulate. **Edward Bethell**

Conclusion: *Rough around the edges as a two-year-old and showed more than enough on his nursery debut at Pontefract to suggest he has plenty of handicapping scope from a BHA mark of 74; will stay 1m+*

Dream of Love (Ire) 108p

3 b.f. Shamardal (USA) – Secret Gesture (Galileo (Ire))
2022 7g* 8s³ :: 2023 7s² Jan 27

Dream of Love enhanced her standing with a very promising run in defeat at the Dubai Carnival in January. The race in question was a valuable seven-furlong conditions event in which the form pick was another Godolphin filly, Mawj, winner of the Duchess of Cambridge Stakes last season from Lezoo and later third to the same filly in the Cheveley Park Stakes. Mawj duly won, but it was a desperately close finish in which Dream of Love had to be considered a very unlucky loser. Racing freely in rear, Dream of Love still had at least 10 lengths to make up on the leaders two furlongs out but finished with a flourish to go down by a short head. As a point of interest, the going on Meydan's turf course was soft, a rare description in those parts after Dubai had their average year's worth of rain in three days!

Dream of Love looked a different proposition in Dubai from her two runs at Newmarket in October, though she had made a good start at her home track. She justified good support to make a winning debut in a fillies' maiden, by a neck under a hands-and-heels ride, and three weeks later was sent off favourite again when stepping up to a mile for the listed Montrose Fillies' Stakes. Dream of Love showed some improvement on the last occasion but not enough to get the better of the more experienced pair Caernarfon and Keep In Touch, who beat her half a length and three quarters of a length. As in Dubai, Dream of Love didn't settle that well and, having got to the front two furlongs out, she was headed soon after.

The way Dream of Love finished at Meydan suggests she ought to be at least as effective back at a mile, but her tendency to race quite freely does raise some doubts about whether she'll stay quite so well as her dam. Secret Gesture was second in the Oaks (also placed in German and Yorkshire Oaks) and a sister to the high-class middle-distance colts from Ballydoyle, Japan and Mogul. While Secret Gesture has produced a couple of middle-distance winners in France by Dubawi, her other winner, Silent Wave, was a useful sprinter by War Front. Whatever her optimum trip proves to be, Dream of Love looks a Group race winner in waiting. **Charlie Appleby**

Conclusion: *Built on two-year-old promise when unlucky to be narrowly beaten by a useful filly in Dubai early in year and looks well up to making amends at a higher level*

Dusky Lord 112

5 b.g. Twilight Son – Petit Trianon (Dansili)
2022 5g* 5g 5m⁴ 5m² 5.4g 6g³ 5.6d 6g* Sep 17

Despite winning twice and making the frame three times in 2022, there remains a feeling that Dusky Lord has yet to reach his full potential and he could well be a sprinter to be reckoned with in 2023, particularly as he has been bought for 70,000 guineas by owner Tom Morley, an astute operator whose previous purchases include the Group 1-winning sprinters Prohibit and Goldream.

Dusky Lord won a Newmarket handicap from a BHA mark of 82 on his seasonal reappearance in May before finishing down the field in the 'Dash' at Epsom on his next start, a run easily excused as he was found to have lost both fore shoes in the rough and tumble of that race. A couple of good runs followed before he trailed in last when fitted with first-time blinkers in a competitive handicap at York's Ebor Festival, having a hopeless task from the position he found himself in. He again wasn't seen to anything like best effect in a similar contest at Goodwood later that month, finishing third after being short of room and unable to fully open up until it was too late. Next up was the Portland at Doncaster where again Dusky Lord failed to get the rub of the green, ending up finishing second in the disadvantaged group that raced up the centre but only tenth overall.

With cheekpieces re-applied (he'd worn them when runner-up at Goodwood in July), Dusky Lord finally had everything go his way when last seen winning the Ayr Silver Cup in September, forging clear to land the spoils by three lengths with the sort of authority that is rarely seen in that sort of handicap. The handicapper has raised him to 99 on the back of that effort, but there is certainly still some room for manoeuvre off that revised mark, and he'll presumably start out for new trainer Stuart Williams in high-end handicaps with a more than competitive chance. It's not hard to see him winning a valuable handicap before making the step up to pattern company. **Stuart Williams**

Conclusion: *Ended last season firmly on the up and could prove a shrewd buy for his new connections with valuable handicaps and pattern races likely on the agenda*

Dusky Lord (white) storms clear of his rivals in the Ayr Silver Cup

Enfjaar (Ire) 94p

3 b.c. Lope de Vega (Ire) – Tesoro (Ire) (Galileo (Ire))
2022 7g* Oct 1

There were a couple of two-year-old maidens on Newmarket's Sun Chariot Stakes card at the beginning of October and the winners of both races have made it into this year's *Fifty*. Charlie Appleby had already won the mile contest with Imperial Emperor and had the odds-on favourite for the seven-furlong event as well with Military Order, a brother to the Derby and King George winner Adayar. The Godolphin colt was one of three well-bred newcomers who headed the market in the field of 10, but it was the other two who fought out a close finish.

A tall colt who was fitted with a hood but who looked the part beforehand and in good order, victory went to the Roger Varian-trained Enfjaar. He took a while to find his full stride but came home well with a neck to spare over Arabian Storm, a colt by Kingman trained by Andrew Balding out of the Juddmonte International winner Arabian Queen. Enfjaar was waited with before being shaken up three furlongs out and began to make headway in the final two furlongs before staying on to head Arabian Storm in the final 50 yards. Bodorgan, the only one of the principals with some experience, stuck to his task after making most of the running to be beaten another half a length in third, with Military Order, who ran green, keeping on to complete the frame. While neither of the first two were turned out again, the form could hardly have worked out better as the next three home all won next time. Bodorgan and Military Order both won novices back at Newmarket later in the month, while the fifth, Laafi, showed improved form when winning a maiden at Nottingham.

Enfjaar was bought by Shadwell for 240,000 guineas as a foal and is his dam's third winner after the seven-furlong/mile winners Sweet Enough and Queenlet, the former also by Enfjaar's sire Lope de Vega. Although by Galileo, their dam Tesoro was speedy enough to win over six furlongs at two, being a granddaughter of the King's Stand Stakes winner Cassandra Go. Enfjaar's wider family is a thriving one and had a couple of important updates in the autumn with wins for Auguste Rodin in the Futurity Trophy and Victoria Road in the Breeders' Cup Juvenile Turf. *Roger Varian*

Conclusion: *Well-bred colt who looks sure to improve on a successful debut in a Newmarket maiden which worked out well*

Fast And Loose 94p

4 b.g. No Nay Never (USA) – Madam Valentine (Primo Valentino (Ire))
2022 t6s³ 6v² 7d 6g 6m² 6m* 6g² 6g 6g² t6s² Oct 18

Fast And Loose has gained his only win to date in a three-runner contest at Catterick—where one of his rivals was a 66/1 shot—but he has already held his own in much more competitive fields and appeals as the type to pick up a good sprint handicap or two this season. He was seen out only once at two, finishing third at Haydock over seven furlongs, but was busier last season when raced mainly over six. Having been placed in his first three career starts, Fast And Loose twice finished down the field in handicaps at York and fared only a little better when picking up more place money from second in a maiden at Ripon.

Fast And Loose was therefore in danger of failing to deliver on his earlier promise, but then came his Catterick race, a novice in July. It might not have been much of a contest, but he did manage to overturn the odds-on Grantley Hall, and it seemed to spark a revival of his fortunes because Fast And Loose fared much better back in handicaps in the second half of the season. The fitting of headgear seemed to be an important factor in his improvement; he wore cheekpieces for the first time at Catterick and then again on his next two starts before blinkers were applied for his last couple of outings.

Once again, Fast And Loose ran no sort of race back at York, but his three other starts in handicaps later in the year all resulted in narrow defeats. Despite a poor draw which resulted in him being ridden much more patiently than usual, Fast And Loose went down by just a head to Corinthia Knight at Pontefract. After his poor run at York, he bounced back at odds of 40/1 12 days later in a huge field for the Ayr Bronze Cup where he went down fighting by a short head to Danzan after showing speed throughout. Fast And Loose went closer still on his final start in a keenly-contested race at Newcastle in October when faring best of those ridden close to a strong pace and edged out only by a nose by Water of Leith. Having gone close in the Bronze Cup, Fast And Loose could be aiming for Silver or even Gold at Ayr later this season. He's versatile in terms of ground. **Kevin Ryan**

Conclusion: *Improved for the fitting of headgear in the latter part of last year when touched off in some competitive sprints and is capable of winning similar events*

David Johnson (Fast And Loose): *"Kevin Ryan has few peers when it comes to training progressive sprint handicappers and Fast And Loose looks just the sort to enhance his record further in 2023. He was a slow burner last year but was runner-up in his last two handicaps, short-headed in the Ayr Bronze Cup and going down by a nose to Water of Leith at Newcastle, doing easily best of those that raced up with the pace in the latter. He's a half-brother to Pipers Note who progressed well at four and five and, if Fast And Loose makes it back to Ayr towards the end of the season, it could be the Silver or Gold Cup he's aiming at."*

Feel The Need   85p

3 b.g. Ribchester (Ire) – Patterned (Dansili)
2022 7.2g⁴ 7.2m* 7g 8g Sep 17

Feel The Need will need to have grown up over the winter—he was slowly away and looked rather green on all four of his outings as a two-year-old—but a gelding operation should help in that regard and, with a bit more maturity on his side, we reckon he's got the makings of a useful handicapper in the North.

Feel The Need showed plenty when fourth on his debut over seven furlongs at Ayr in July, and he confirmed that promise when getting off the mark over the same course and distance a fortnight later, doing well to quicken past his rivals from off a steady gallop. It's maybe a clue to the regard in which Feel The Need is held that David O'Meara ran him in the Group 3 Acomb Stakes at York on his next start and, while he wasn't up to that level, he didn't run badly in seventh in a hot contest won by the subsequent Dewhurst Stakes winner Chaldean. Feel The Need went back to Ayr for a one-mile nursery on his final start, and the bare facts of him beating just two in ninth don't tell the full story. Another sluggish start left him with a lot to do, but he still looked full of running in last when getting chopped off under two furlongs out and Danny Tudhope understandably wasn't hard on him after. That run suggested Feel The Need should be competitive from a BHA mark of 85 another time, not least once he learns to race more professionally.

A lengthy gelding, Feel The Need is the type to do well physically from two to three and, as a son of Ribchester from a family cultivated at the Cumani's Fittocks Stud, he should have little trouble staying at least a mile. **David O'Meara**

Conclusion: *Green and probably only scratching the surface in four runs at two; looks the type to thrive in well-run handicaps at around 1m in 2023*

Greek Order   87p

3 b.c. Kingman – Trojan Queen (USA) (Empire Maker (USA))
2022 7g³ 7d² Oct 19

Roger Charlton trained winners for the late Khalid Abdullah for 30 years, starting from 1990 when Charlton completed a Derby double at Epsom and Chantilly with the Abdullah colts Quest For Fame and Sanglamore in his first season with the licence at Beckhampton. Things are a little different nowadays, with Charlton sharing that licence with son Harry from early last year, while following Abdullah's death in early-2021—"I owe him everything" said Charlton at the time—the Abdullah horses now race under the Juddmonte banner. But the successful partnership between Beckhampton and Juddmonte lives on as shown at Royal Ascot last year when the Charltons had their first joint-winner at the meeting with Thesis in the Britannia Stakes.

It's not out of the question that Greek Order could be a Royal Ascot type himself. After all, he's by the same sire as Thesis, Kingman, and is a brother to another Royal Ascot winner, Sangarius, who struck in the Hampton Court Stakes in 2019. Sangarius was a listed winner at two for Sir Michael Stoute and thought worthy of contesting the Dewhurst Stakes, whereas Greek Order starts his three-year-old season still a maiden, though it shouldn't take him long to shed that tag. Greek Order was strongly fancied to make a winning debut in a novice at Salisbury in September, sent off the 6/4 favourite, but proved too green against a couple of more experienced rivals. Still, he shaped well in being beaten a length into third behind Secret Solace and Havana Blue without being given too hard a race.

The following month at Newmarket, Greek Order went closer in a similar event but still showed signs of inexperience, running green once hitting the front over a furlong out and then headed in the final 50 yards as he went down by a neck to Godolphin's odds-on favourite Regal Honour. Nonetheless, Greek Order shaped encouragingly again and, being a tall colt with scope for more progress at three, he seems sure to win races this year. A very smart winner at up to a mile and a quarter, Sangarius is the pick of several winners among Greek Order's siblings, while one of his half-sisters is the dam of last year's Prix Jean-Luc Lagardère winner Belbek. This is one of the finest Juddmonte families, with Greek Order having high-class filly Banks Hill, herself a Royal Ascot winner in the Coronation Stakes, as his grandam. **Harry & Roger Charlton**

Conclusion: *Juddmonte colt bred in the purple who went close in both his starts at two despite showing signs of greenness and well up to winning races this year with further improvement to come*

Hickory (Ire) 99p

5 b.g. Free Eagle (Ire) – Badr Al Badoor (Ire) (Acclamation)
2022 p7s* p7s* :: 2023 t7.1f⁴ Feb 23

Winning newcomers from the James Fanshawe yard are quite rare and tend to prove useful, so expectations for Hickory would no doubt have been high following his successful debut at Yarmouth in August 2020, not least considering the style in which he did it, quickening from last to first to win by a length and a quarter in ready fashion. It was presumably quite a serious problem that then kept him off the track until October last year, but the way he landed short odds in a novice at Kempton suggested all his ability remained intact and, encouragingly, he showed no ill effects when making a winning handicap debut over the same course and distance seven weeks later. An opening mark of 80 proved woefully inadequate that day—he only won by three quarters of a length but was value for extra having been eased late on—and it's doubtful a subsequent 7 lb rise will be anything like enough to stop him winning again.

Admittedly, Hickory was unable to defy his revised mark at the first attempt—he lost his unbeaten record when fourth on his first start of 2023 at Southwell in February—but he wasn't seen to best effect in a messy race and remains with plenty of potential intact for the season ahead. Fanshawe knows Hickory's family well, having trained both the dam and half-sister, both of whom were useful sprinters. Hickory is by Prince of Wales's Stakes winner Free Eagle, who has seemingly injected a bit more stamina into the mix, with his four starts all coming over seven furlongs. He's likely to stay a mile, like his full-brother Hover, but certainly isn't short of speed and there'll probably be no hurry to get him up in trip, his strong-travelling style making him the ideal type for the straight course at Ascot, where there's no shortage of good seven-furlong handicaps. **James Fanshawe**

Conclusion: *Lightly-raced five-year-old who remains with potential despite meeting with his first defeat at Southwell, seemingly possessing all the tools to develop into a high-end handicapper*

Hi Royal (Ire) 88p

3 b.c. Kodiac – Majestic Roi (USA) (Street Cry (Ire))
2022 7m³ 8g* Sep 15

An SP of 50/1 suggests not many backed Hi Royal when he made his debut in a valuable maiden at York's Ebor Festival in August, but those who did could have been forgiven for writing off all hope as the newcomer toiled in rear, looking clueless, for the first half of the race. That Hi Royal ended up being beaten just half a length and a short head into third behind Godolphin's odds-on favourite, Desert Order, and Glenfinnan—both of whom had experience to call upon and were up with the pace throughout—in a 17-strong field says plenty, therefore, about how the second half of his race unfolded.

That eye-catching beginning wasn't just a case of style over substance, either, as Desert Order started almost as short in a Newmarket nursery on his next and final outing and ran to a high level in defying an opening BHA mark of 92, at the chief expense of a stablemate who'd made a sound start to his own career. For his part, Hi Royal was seen again only once and didn't disappoint as he proved in a different league to his nine rivals in a novice event at Ayr in September, striding to a two-and-a-half length win in ready fashion, already well clear when eased late on.

That Hi Royal proved his stamina for a mile so early in his first year might suggest he'll flourish over middle-distances in 2023—his siblings include a smart winner at up to a mile and a half in the shape of Noor Al Hawa (by Makfi)—but he looked a strong-travelling sort at Ayr and may prove best when the emphasis is more on speed. By Kodiac and out of the Sun Chariot Stakes winner Majestic Roi, Hi Royal is one to look out for in high-end three-year-old handicaps at around a mile. ***Kevin Ryan***

Conclusion: *Showed plenty of ability in two juvenile starts and has an excellent pedigree which underpins his potential heading into 2023*

Imperial Emperor (Ire) 96P

3 b.c. Dubawi (Ire) – Zhukova (Ire) (Fastnet Rock (Aus))
2022 8g* Oct 1

Timeform's Horse of the Year in 2020 after reeling off a hat-trick of Group 1 wins in the Coronation Cup at Newmarket (moved from Epsom due to the Covid-19 pandemic), Coral-Eclipse at Sandown and Juddmonte International at York, Ghaiyyath didn't reach his peak until his five-year-old season, but there is hope that his close relation, Imperial Emperor, could develop into a leading classic contender in 2023 judged on the impression he created on his sole two-year-old start.

Like Ghaiyyath before him, Imperial Emperor is trained by Charlie Appleby and the maiden he won at Newmarket in October is a race his stable has often targeted with a good prospect. For example, Appleby won the 2017 running with Old Persian, who later developed into a very smart performer over middle-distances, notably winning the 2019 Dubai Sheema Classic. Appleby also struck in 2020 with the useful Mystical Dawn before Al Nafir was forced to settle for the runner-up spot 12 months later. A full brother to none other than Ghaiyyath, Al Nafir is another entry in this year's *Fifty* having ended last season with a career-best effort to win the Old Rowley Cup back at Newmarket.

Admittedly, the latest edition of that maiden probably wasn't the strongest race of its type—only six runners went to post and the four to have raced since have all failed to get off the mark—but there was plenty to like about the style of the winner's performance. Settled just behind the leaders in the early stages, Imperial Emperor moved up to lead entering the final two furlongs and gradually drew clear from there, ultimately winning by three and a half lengths with plenty in hand.

Not only does Imperial Emperor share his sire with Ghaiyyath (both by Dubawi), but his dam, Zhukova, also happens to be a half-sister to that top-class performer. Ghaiyyath and Zhukova are both out of the Galileo mare Nightime, who won the 2006 Irish 1000 Guineas for Dermot Weld. Weld also trained Zhukova in her racing days, with the highlight of her career coming in 2017 when she won the Grade 1 Man o'War Stakes in the US. Imperial Emperor is her second foal after First Ruler (also by Dubawi), who was fifth behind Al Nafir in last season's Old Rowley Cup and has since shown smart form when winning a handicap at Meydan.

A sturdy colt, Imperial Emperor is open to significant improvement, especially as his stamina is drawn out further. He is likely to stay a mile and a half and will surely have a Derby trial on his agenda in the spring, very much the type to go on to bigger and better things. **Charlie Appleby**

Conclusion: *Bred in the purple and created an excellent impression on debut; has scope for plenty of improvement and looks a likely type for a Derby trial*

Infinite Cosmos (Ire)   86P

3 ch.f. Sea The Stars (Ire) – Waila (Notnowcato)
2022 8v² Oct 21

Infinite Cosmos was one of the biggest eyecatchers of the autumn when finishing a close second on her debut at Doncaster in October and, as a choicely-bred filly in some of the best possible hands, she's an absolute no-brainer inclusion in this year's *Fifty*. Greenness was the only thing that cost Infinite Cosmos a winning debut on Town Moor as a slow start left her in a poor position out wide and towards the rear. She made striking headway entering the final furlong and was closing down the experienced winner Sea of Roses all the way to the line, ultimately passing the post just a short head behind that rival and showing fairly useful form in the process.

That debut effort bore all the hallmarks of a filly sure to improve plenty for the experience and that's without considering a pedigree and profile that screams better three-year-old. Infinite Cosmos is from a line that has served Sir Michael Stoute and the Rothschild family very well over the years, featuring as it does a number of smart or better performers, notably the Prince of Wales's Stakes winner Crystal Ocean, who is out of a half-sister to Infinite Cosmos' dam Waila, herself a smart performer at up to a mile and three-quarters. Like Crystal Ocean, Infinite Cosmos is by Sea The Stars, so there's top-class middle-distance blood on both sides of her pedigree, and there can be no doubt that she's going to prove at her best over a mile and a quarter and beyond. Winning a maiden or novice early in the season should be a formality, and it wouldn't be any surprise at all to see her on the Oaks trail by the end of the spring. **Sir Michael Stoute**

Conclusion: *Shaped very well amidst greenness on her sole juvenile start and looks the type to step up massively over middle distances as a three-year-old*

Ingra Tor (Ire) 97

4 b.g. Churchill (Ire) – Kassia (Ire) (Acclamation)
2022 t6.1g* p6s² 6g* 6m 6m 7m² 6g³ 6d³ Aug 26

It's fair to say that Ingra Tor's three-year-old campaign failed to deliver on its early promise, but he is not one to give up on just yet and remains a sprint handicapper to follow in his first season with Jack Channon now at the helm at West Ilsley.

Ingra Tor finished down the field at Newmarket on his sole start at two, when the market suggested he was quite highly thought of, and he wasted little time showing why he'd attracted that support when winning a novice at Southwell on his return the following March. Beaten a neck in a similar event at Kempton next time which proved good form, Ingra Tor continued his progress when making a successful handicap debut at Newmarket on 2000 Guineas day. He proved to be thrown in as he took a strong-looking race in good style, travelling well behind the pace before quickening to lead over a furlong out, ultimately winning by two and a quarter lengths from Harry Three in dominant fashion. The time of the race backed up the good visual impression created by Ingra Tor and he looked all set for further success.

Indeed, Ingra Tor started a strong favourite to beat Harry Three (who had won at Newmarket in the meantime) again when they reopposed in the valuable three-year-old handicap on York's Macmillan Charity Raceday in June. But while Harry Three won well with a smart performance before going on to complete a hat-trick in a listed race at

Ingra Tor in winning action at Newmarket

Deauville, Ingra Tor, who'd had the race as his long-term target, seemingly had no excuses in finishing in mid-division.

Ingra Tor's four remaining starts all took place on Newmarket's July Course. He was backed to make amends in another valuable three-year-old handicap at the July Festival but finished down the field again, though this time his draw and track position offered a plausible excuse. Although picking up place money in small fields in his last three races, Ingra Tor was mainly disappointing. The best of those runs came when second of five to Love de Vega over seven furlongs, but he was too keen early on and didn't see his race out fully as a result, while softer ground may not have suited on his final start. **Jack Channon**

Conclusion: *Looked a three-year-old sprinter going places last spring before disappointing later on; had excuses for some of those runs and could be the type to resume progress after a break since last summer*

Kintaro   76p
3 b.c. Iffraaj – Soryah (Ire) (Shamardal (USA))
2022 7.9d⁴ Oct 8

A useful handicapper at his best, Smart Champion was finally back among the winners last season with victories at Beverley in July and Kempton in September, ending a losing run stretching back to his sole previous win for the David Simcock stable at Newcastle in February 2020. Smart Champion is the first—and, as it stands, best—foal out of the useful middle-distance handicapper Soryah, but the likeable veteran could soon face competition on that score from his youngest sibling in training, such was the impression created by Richard Fahey's Kintaro when he finished fourth at 20/1 in a York maiden in October.

That York contest was won by another newcomer in the shape of Martyn Meade's strong-travelling Modesty, ahead of the pair with the best form, but it was Kintaro who impressed most among the also-rans, getting the hang of things late on and very much taking the eye with his finishing effort. Beaten just three and three-quarter lengths at the line, having been outpaced early in the straight, he shaped like a horse who will flourish when tackling middle-distances as a three-year-old and his pedigree certainly gives cause for plenty of optimism in that regard. Smart Champion, for example, is campaigned almost exclusively in staying handicaps these days and their half-sister, Majestic Jewel, notched her only win the first time she was stepped up to two miles on soft ground.

Kintaro is a banker to win a maiden or novice when upped in trip in 2023 and, if the consistency and durability of his premier relative is any guide, he is likely to have no difficulty making his presence felt in the more demanding environment of three-year-old handicaps sooner rather than later. **Richard Fahey**

Conclusion: *Stoutly-bred sort who is open to plenty of improvement after merely scratching the surface of his ability and stamina when a fast-finishing fourth in a well-contested York maiden; will stay 1¼m+*

Kyle of Lochalsh 76p
3 b.c. Highland Reel (Ire) – Quiz Mistress (Doyen (Ire))
2022 p8s p8s p10s⁵ Dec 22

Kyle of Lochalsh is a picturesque village on the north-west coast of Scotland located on the Lochalsh peninsula that, along with the nearby village of Plockton, was used as the backdrop for the BBC drama series Hamish Macbeth. It's also proving to be a popular name for racehorses, the latest recipient hopefully destined for greater success than the gelding of the same name who ended his career for Lucinda Russell in 2007 with a series of miserable efforts under both codes.

The latest Kyle of Lochalsh has the look of a colt who will do well in middle-distance handicaps as a three-year-old. He had a trio of runs on the all-weather towards the backend of 2022, running his best race when upped to a mile and a quarter for a novice event at Lingfield on the final one. The winner of that race Nazymbek is a smashing prospect, while Kyle of Lochalsh did more than enough to believe that an opening BHA mark of 71 probably underplays his ability, especially as he'll surely be more at home when faced with a stiffer test of stamina. His pedigree certainly suggests that will be the case—his dam Quiz Mistress was a smart performer at up to a mile and three-quarters and his year-older half-brother Wagga Wagga was progressive over middle-distances in 2022 despite being notably headstrong.

Kyle of Lochalsh is just the sort of horse that Hughie Morrison can typically be expected to improve as a three-year-old, and though Highland Reel has made a rather quiet start to his career at stud it wouldn't be a huge surprise if his progeny are slower-maturing types by and large.

With his oldest runners having only just turned four, there's plenty of time for him to start siring horses more in the image of himself. *Hughie Morrison*

Conclusion: *Was going the right way in three qualifying runs on the all-weather and should prove capable of better when tackling middle-distance/staying handicaps; will stay 1¼m+*

Laurel

117p

4 b.f. Kingman – Promising Lead (Danehill (USA))
2022 8m* p8s* 8g² Oct 1

Arguably unlucky not to win the Oaks at Epsom, where she was beaten just a short head by Tuesday despite having stumbled leaving the stalls, Emily Upjohn did eventually make the breakthrough in Group 1 company when landing the Fillies' & Mares' Stakes at Ascot, in doing so matching the feats of stable companions Inspiral, winner of the Coronation Stakes, and Nashwa, successful in the Prix de Diane and Nassau Stakes. The Gosden operation's hand in the top fillies' events would be further complemented by the later-developing Laurel, who didn't see a racecourse until late-July but was fast-tracked into the Sun Chariot Stakes on just her third career start after bloodless victories in novice events at Newmarket and Kempton.

Supplemented for the Sun Chariot at a fee of £20,000, that Group 1 coming only 10 days after her Kempton success, Laurel shaped very well despite forfeiting her unbeaten record on the Rowley Mile, just her lack of experience costing her victory after she'd looked to come with a winning run. She was headed again in the final 50 yards by the rallying Fonteyn, ultimately passing the post three quarters of a length behind that rival but leaving with her burgeoning reputation enhanced.

A strong-travelling sort who has raced exclusively at a mile to date, Laurel retains huge potential heading into her second season. A rangy, attractive filly, she is in the very best of hands and the option of longer trips seems likely to be explored sooner rather than later, with the Dahlia Stakes at Newmarket and/or the Middleton Stakes at York appealing as suitable early-season targets. Beyond that, she'll surely be mixing it at the top level once again before too long, perhaps even following in the footsteps of her dam, who won the Middleton on her first outing as a four-year-old before crossing the

Irish Sea to take the Pretty Polly Stakes at the Curragh on what would prove to be her final start. **John & Thady Gosden**

Conclusion: *Looked potentially something out of the ordinary when winning her first two starts and her scope for more improvement suggests she won't be long in making amends for a narrow reverse in the Sun Chariot*

La Yakel   **104p**

4 b.g. Time Test – Tebee's Oasis (Oasis Dream)
2022 8.3g³ 8.1m³ t11.1g* 12g* 12g⁴ Oct 7

Time Test might have fallen below the very top level as a racehorse—third behind Hawkbill in the 2016 Eclipse was his best attempt when tried in Group 1 company in Britain—but his impeccable pedigree meant he was always likely to be in demand as a sire and the early signs are that he's going to provide a good-value angle for those breeders who want a proven middle-distance Juddmonte family but are a long way from affording Frankel's stud fee.

La Yakel (yellow) is likely to progress further after just five starts

Highly progressive in five starts as a three-year-old having been unraced as a juvenile, La Yakel will hopefully prove to be a flagbearer for his sire in 2023. He put up his best performance to date when defying a BHA mark of 87 in a valuable three-year-old handicap over a mile and a half at Ascot in September, swooping through from off the pace to lead inside the final 100 yards. The official winning margin was just half a length, but he was arguably value for extra having come from further back than the pair he pulled clear with, those in behind featuring a whole host of useful or better types from powerful yards. And though unable to defy a 5 lb rise when favourite for the Old Rowley Cup at Newmarket the following month, La Yakel was hardly disgraced in coming home fourth of the 16 runners in another really strong-looking handicap, doing more than enough to confirm earlier impressions that he'll do better again as a four-year-old.

The William Haggas yard often targets the Jorvik Handicap at York's Dante Festival with a lightly-raced improver, notably winning the race with Ilaraab in 2021 and Gaassee in 2022, both four-year-olds in these colours. All things being equal, La Yakel looks an ideal type to start his 2023 campaign in the very same contest, no surprise if he progresses into something that bit better than a handicapper further down the line. **William Haggas**

Conclusion: *Showed up well in two of the most competitive three-year-old handicaps run throughout 2022 and remains open to improvement after just five starts*

Lucky Fifteen (Fr) 58p

3 ch.g. Lope de Vega (Ire) – Bess of Hardwick (Dansili)
2022 8v⁶ p7s t7.2d⁶ Nov 7

On the face of it, Lucky Fifteen proved a disappointment last year as he failed to improve from his Sandown debut in two subsequent starts, including when sent off favourite for a novice event at Kempton in October. However, there's plenty to recommend him as the sort to do better in middle-distance handicaps—especially with a winter and a gelding operation behind him—and he appeals as the type to rack up a sequence starting out from a lowly mark.

Lucky Fifteen ran arguably his worst race yet at Kempton, but the money that came for him on that occasion suggests he is clearly thought capable of better. A well-backed 9/4 favourite dropped to seven furlongs, he lacked the early speed to take up a prominent position and was never able to land a blow having been pushed along on the home turn. It was a similar story at Wolverhampton next time, though he was at least able to sit closer to the speed before a wide trip seemed to take its toll in the straight, ultimately passing the post eight lengths behind the winner in sixth.

An expensive yearling at 200,000 guineas, Lucky Fifteen is bred to be suited by at least a mile and a quarter, certainly on the distaff of his pedigree—his dam was a winner at up to 13 furlongs and her half-brother, Ask, won twice at Group 1 level in the Coronation Cup over a mile and a half and the Prix Royal-Oak over nearly two miles. Only time will tell just how far Lucky Fifteen will stay, but there should be plenty more to come from him as a three-year-old when he gets the opportunity to tackle middle-distance handicaps. He is likely to prove better than a BHA mark of 64 and it might take the handicapper a while to catch up with him if he gets rolling early in the season. *Ralph Beckett*

Conclusion: *Looked a work in progress in three starts at two and should leave that form well behind in 2023, as befits one with his useful middle-distance pedigree (bred to be suited by 1¼m+)*

Manaccan 122

4 ch.c. Exceed And Excel (Aus) – Shyrl (Acclamation)
2022 6g 5m⁵ 5.1g² 5m* 6d³ 5g* 5.2g³ 5d* p5g* Oct 21

It's fair to say that Manaccan—who takes his name from a village on the Lizard Peninsula in the southern part of Cornwall—didn't exactly hit the ground running as a two-year-old having been bought for 100,000 guineas at the breeze-ups in April that year, though he did run out an easy winner when opening his account at the third attempt in a novice event at Newmarket.

Starting out in sprint handicaps early last season, Manaccan shaped well in five-furlong events at Royal Ascot and Chester before getting off the mark for the campaign at the Shergar Cup. He would go on to win three more races at that trip before the season had drawn to a conclusion, culminating in a Group 3 win at Dundalk, his trainer's first at that level since Iver Bridge Lad struck in the Prix de Seine-Et-Oise at Maisons–Laffitte in late-2011. At Dundalk, Manaccan was sent off the even-money favourite—despite being up against several smart rivals who already had course form—and he duly produced a career-best effort to round off a most successful season, angling out early in the straight and pouncing late on land the spoils by half a length from Logo Hunter.

While his penultimate victory in the listed Rous Stakes at Ascot was gained on good to soft going, which proved his effectiveness with some ease in the ground, Manaccan is all about speed and a sound surface ought to play more to his strengths. He still has some ground to make up on the likes of Highfield Princess, who improved at a rate of knots herself last season, completing a hat-trick of wins in Group 1 sprints during August and September, but there must be a good chance that the best is still to come from him this year. Very much a sprinter going places, Manaccan will be one to look

Manaccan (yellow) looks a sprinter going places

out for in races such as the Palace House Stakes at Newmarket and Temple Stakes at Haydock during the first part of the 2023 campaign. *John Ryan*

Conclusion: *Developed into a very smart sprinter last season, culminating in a Group 3 success at Dundalk, and promises to have another productive campaign in 2023; has form at 6f but seems best at 5f*

Mount Athos 109p

4 b.c. Dark Angel (Ire) – Ceaseless (Ire) (Iffraaj)
2022 7g² 7m⁴ 7m* p7s* Oct 19

Mount Athos looks an unexposed four-year-old to have on your side in 2023 when he could easily develop into something a bit better than a handicapper. Unraced at two, he made his debut last season in a novice at Doncaster's Lincoln meeting where he shaped well after a slow break, taking the eye with how he moved through the contest and briefly threatening to give the winner Dawn of Liberation a real race. In the end, he had to settle for second, three lengths behind the winner, but looked sure to progress. It was early-June before Mount Athos was seen out again, when returned to Doncaster for a similar event, and while he only ran to a similar level as on his debut, he wasn't given too hard a race once held in fourth behind some useful rivals, with runner-up Thesis going on to win the Britannia Stakes at Royal Ascot later in the month.

There was a much shorter gap to Mount Athos's third start as it came just 10 days later at Thirsk when he got off the mark in ready fashion in another novice. Despite an awkward start, he was soon travelling best in the lead and quickened clear from two furlongs out to win easily by five lengths from Conflict, who ran up a hat-trick later in the year and is now a useful performer in Qatar. Once again, Mount Athos was off the track for a while after his Thirsk victory but returned with a much-improved effort on his handicap debut at Kempton in September. Sent off the 2/1 favourite, that evidently wasn't unexpected, and he showed himself to be well ahead of his opening BHA mark of 84. Travelling smoothly at the head of affairs once again, Mount Athos quickened clear over two furlongs out for an impressive five-length win over Top Secret, who went on to win his next two races at the same track.

Mount Athos has raced only at seven furlongs and isn't really bred to get much further as his dam won a maiden at the same trip for the same connections, though she earned some black type from finishing second in a listed race in Germany over nine furlongs. James Tate made a good start to the year on the all-weather and Mount Athos seems sure to give his stable further success in 2023. *James Tate*

Conclusion: *Had a stop-start campaign in 2022 but ended it with an impressive win on his handicap debut and, still unexposed, looks likely to win more races as a smart four-year-old*

 # Mr Buster (Ire) 86p
3 br.c. Sea The Stars (Ire) – Olympienne (Ire) (Sadler's Wells (USA))
2022 8.3v^2 p8s^3 Oct 31

The pale blue colours of Ballymacoll Stud with a yellow and white cap were carried to success in no fewer than 55 Group 1 races over the last 60 or so years, including by Derby winners Troy and North Light, and it was the end of an era when the whole operation was broken up and sold in 2017. That did, however, give breeders access to some of the finest families in the stud book and the one going back to 1990 Yorkshire Oaks winner Hellenic was one of Ballymacoll's best. Four-time Group 1 winner Islington is the pick of the family in terms of what she achieved on the track, but as a broodmare she's been surpassed by her year-younger half-sister Olympienne. The very smart stayer Patkai—runner-up to Yeats in a Gold Cup and described by Sir Michael Stoute in a recent interview with Racing TV as "the best 'Cup' horse I ever had"—is the pick of Olympienne's progeny to date, and while the Ralph Beckett-trained Mr Buster has a way to go to reach that level, two runs as a juvenile suggests he's got all the makings of a really useful three-year-old stayer.

Given the late-maturing nature of his family, it's no surprise that Mr Buster wasn't seen out until October, and he showed lots of ability in finishing second in a novice event at Nottingham and third in a maiden at Kempton, despite leaving the impression neither race tested his stamina sufficiently. Indeed, Mr Buster looks absolutely certain to relish middle-distances and beyond judged on both sides of his pedigree—he's a son of the great Sea The Stars—and, considering he's already reached a fairly useful level of form, that makes him a most interesting prospect for 2023. He needs another run for a mark, but his form is already good enough to win a maiden or novice event, and he strongly appeals as the type to keep on improving as his stamina is drawn out further over the course of the season. **Ralph Beckett**

Conclusion: *Showed plenty in a couple of runs at two and has a smart, stamina-laden pedigree which suggests there'll be considerable progress to come as he matures at three; will be suited by 1¼m+*

Naomi Lapaglia   84p
3 b.f. Awtaad (Ire) – Hawaafez (Nayef (USA))
2022 p8s* Nov 9

Naomi Lapaglia, played by Margot Robbie, was the title character's wife in The Wolf of Wall Street, a Hollywood blockbuster that earned five Academy Award nominations. The equine Naomi Lapaglia is also expected to earn rave reviews as her career progresses.

A cheap yearling at just 2,000 guineas, Naomi Lapaglia clearly progressed well physically in a short space of time as she was sold again for 110,000 guineas as a two-year-old, though it wasn't until well into the second half of the campaign before she appeared on a racecourse for the first time. That debut came in a fillies' novice event at Kempton in November where she was sent off at 14/1 in a 14-strong field. Drawn in stall two, she missed the break but recovered quickly to race in touch and was still on the bridle when produced to lead around two furlongs out. Tackled inside the final furlong, by a well-touted newcomer from the Gosden stable, she was always holding on and ultimately won by half a length in comfortable fashion.

That was a most promising start to Naomi Lapaglia's career, especially as she's very much bred to come into her own at three, her half-sister Rogue Millennium having won last year's Lingfield Oaks Trial a mere two weeks on from her own successful debut. Naomi Lapaglia probably won't be set such a stiff task on her second start, but she promises to make up into a useful filly in her own right and seems sure to relish middle-distances in time, her dam a smart sort who won the Cumberland Lodge Stakes and stayed at least 13 furlongs. **Richard Spencer**

Conclusion: *Looked a useful prospect when making a winning debut at Kempton and seems sure to progress and win more races when tackling middle-distances*

Nights Over Egypt (Ire)   82

3 b.c. Oasis Dream – Beychella (USA) (Scat Daddy (USA))
2022 7d⁴ 7g⁴ 7.8m⁵ 8d³ Oct 17

Rookie trainer James Horton made a highly promising start in 2022, particularly with his three-year-old runners. For context, that age group was responsible for six of his 18 winners and, overall, they operated at a healthy strike rate of 23%, something which bodes well for the prospects of Nights Over Egypt in 2023 following a relatively low-key two-year-old campaign.

Fourth on his debut in a novice event at Haydock in June, passing the post only two and a quarter lengths behind the winner despite showing signs of inexperience, Nights Over Egypt then failed to improve on that effort on his next two starts in similar events, leaving the impression that he was still learning on the job and that there would be more to come when he was qualified for nurseries. That certainly proved to be the case as Nights Over Egypt then showed improved form and shaped well when last seen finishing third on his nursery debut at Pontefract in October. Having travelled smoothly in behind the leaders, he stuck to his task well to be beaten just a length and a quarter and arguably deserved extra credit having raced closer to the pace than the pair who beat him, including the runner-up, Coverdale, who also features in the *Fifty* having shown up so well in a contest which looks strong form for the grade.

An expensive yearling at 140,000 guineas (having previously sold for 40,000 guineas as a foal), Nights Over Egypt certainly looks the part on paper, boasting a useful pedigree—he is by Oasis Dream and from the family of the 1000 Guineas winner Sleepytime on the dam's side—and the physique to suggest he can go on improving this season. He produced his best effort at two when stepping up to a mile and that trip looks an ideal starting point for his three-year-old campaign. A BHA mark of 78 is highly unlikely to prove his limit when he reappears in handicaps in the North for his up-and-coming yard. **James Horton**

Conclusion: *Achieved a fairly useful level of form in four starts at two and probably hasn't finished improving yet with a view to handicaps at around 1m in the North*

Nostrum   112p

3 b.c. Kingman – Mirror Lake (Dubai Destination (USA))
2022 7g* 7g* 7g³ Oct 8

It's a measure of how exciting Nostrum looked in winning his first two starts that he was sent off joint favourite for the Dewhurst Stakes at Newmarket in October. Before that he'd shaped with abundant promise when making a successful debut in a maiden at Sandown in July, overcoming greenness to win by three lengths in impressive fashion, and it was a similar story when he followed up in the Tattersalls Stakes over the Dewhurst course and distance in September, again looking very much in need of the experience but running on well to beat Holloway Boy by a length and a quarter. And though Nostrum came unstuck when bidding to maintain his unbeaten record in the Dewhurst, finishing only third behind Chaldean, beaten two and a quarter lengths, perhaps it was that lack of experience rather than ability which finally found him out. Either way, he's certainly got all the attributes to resume his progress and make a mark at the top level as a three-year-old.

Nostrum has the pedigree of a smart performer—his dam reached that level at around a mile and a quarter, as did his half-brothers Imaging and Titus—and he's even more striking in terms of looks, a strong, good sort who promises to thrive physically as a three-year-old. It's more than 20 years since Golan provided Sir Michael Stoute with the most recent of his five 2,000 Guineas wins, but Nostrum will surely have his attentions turned that way in the spring, and if he improves as much over the winter as we suspect, it's not fanciful to suggest he could make the jump to that level. He's raced at seven furlongs so far but will have no trouble with a mile, and a race such as the Craven Stakes will provide an ideal opportunity for him to test his classic credentials in the early part of the season. *Sir Michael Stoute*

Conclusion: *Outstanding physical specimen who quickly reached a smart level as a juvenile and is in some of the best possible hands to realise his considerable potential at three; will stay 1m*

Novel Legend (Ire) 92

4 b.g. Nathaniel (Ire) – Majestic Dubawi (Dubawi (Ire))
2022 10.2g 11.5g⁶ 10.2g 12g² t12.4s⁴ 14.4d* 16d² Oct 28

"Prize money is next to nothing while training cost is comparable or higher than Australia. Why would anyone want to own a horse there, I keep asking myself." That was the damning verdict on British racing's current parlous state by wealthy Hong Kong-based owner Bon Ho in a rare Twitter post published in late-May. Ironically, Ho's silks were to prove a far more regular sight on Britain's racecourses during the remainder of 2022 than the owner himself on Twitter, his increased presence on these shores seeing him better his tally of winners for 2020 and 2021 put together. That return will hopefully persuade the ambitious owner to maintain his interest in Europe for a bit longer, one which complements the sizeable string of horses he's already amassed in Hong Kong and Australia, the vast majority of whom run under the "Legend" moniker.

Novel Legend may not be up to providing Ho with an elusive first success in the Melbourne Cup—Deauville Legend was fourth for him when sent off favourite in 2022—but he still appeals as one of the owner's British contingent worth following in 2023, when staying trips are likely to be firmly on the agenda despite the speed on the distaff side of his pedigree. His dam Majestic Dubawi was a dual six-furlong winner as a two-year-old, while her three previous winning offspring have all plied their trade over trips ranging from five to seven furlongs, notably the useful performer Isabella Giles (by Belardo). By contrast, Novel Legend takes far more after his sire Nathaniel, a view which had presumably revealed itself fully on James Fanshawe's gallops as, having been unraced at two, he made his debut over a mile and a quarter in a novice event at Nottingham in May.

Novel Legend's three qualifying runs were all about gaining experience and he's made the frame on all four starts since switching to handicaps, his form improving every time he went up in trip. There was plenty to like about Novel Legend's sole win to date, displaying a most willing attitude to land a mile-and-three-quarter handicap at Chester in September, only winning by a neck but deserving extra credit having overcome a troubled passage from much further back than the other principals. Novel Legend lost little in defeat when last seen tackling two miles for the first time at Newmarket in October, staying on well to be beaten just a neck, and he appeals as one Fanshawe can place to advantage from a BHA mark of just 81 in the spring. **James Fanshawe**

Conclusion: *Signed off last season with a career-best effort when stepped up to 2m at Newmarket and looks every inch the type to win more handicaps for this yard as a four-year-old*

Simon Walker (Novel Legend): *"He/she can train anything' is a phrase regularly heard when trainers are touting for business. Well, James Fanshawe has a wealth of results stretching back more than 30 years that proves he can indeed train anything. From Champion Hurdlers to top-notch sprinters and everything in between, Fanshawe is a trainer that places his horses with careful consideration, his campaigning of Novel Legend to date smacking of an anticipation that there are several staying handicaps to be won with him as a four-year-old. Don't be surprised if he's not already earmarked for the Chester Plate or the two-mile handicap at the Dante Meeting."*

Okeechobee clears away from his rivals at Salisbury

Okeechobee 112p

4 b.c. Time Test – Scuffle (Daylami (Ire))
2022 t9.5s² p8s* t9.5s* 9.9g* Sep 29

The Charltons kept things fairly low-key with Okeechobee in 2022, running him just four times, but there was no mistaking his quality and that patient approach is one that should pay dividends this season when he looks all over the type to develop into a pattern-class performer.

Okeechobee is certainly bred to be just that as a half-brother by Time Test to a number of smart or better performers, chief among them the 2019 St Leger winner Logician, and his form is fast heading in that direction as well. He made a really promising debut in a novice event at Wolverhampton in April, when he would have won but for hanging across the track, and he confirmed that promise in striking style at Kempton three months later, when running out a wide-margin winner over a mile. Okeechobee then doubled his tally in straightforward fashion when winning another novice event back at Wolverhampton two weeks later, justifying odds of 20/1-on as he dismissed his sole rival, and he signed off for the season with his best and most substantial performance yet when making a winning handicap debut over a mile and a quarter at Salisbury at the end of September. There were only four runners in that race, but that's not to say it was a weak contest—the runner-up Educator was another progressive three-year-old—and Okeechobee was full value for a smart effort in winning it by four and a quarter lengths.

A subsequent 10 lb rise in the weights to a BHA mark of 102 is unlikely to stop Okeechobee winning more handicaps in 2023 if connections so choose, but it's likely they'll have grander designs at some point and his form is already good enough to go close at listed level, with plenty more improvement surely on the cards. He's raced at up to a mile and a quarter so far and has been rather keen in his races, but his pedigree does suggest he'll stay further as he matures. **Harry & Roger Charlton**

Conclusion: *Half-brother to a St Leger winner and really looked the part when winning three of his four starts as a three-year-old; will surely have pattern races in his sights in 2023*

Rathgar   82p

3 ch.c. Ulysses (Ire) – Why We Dream (Ire) (Al Kazeem)
2022 8g⁶ 9.9g³ 9.1g* Oct 9

Mick Channon celebrated a notable milestone during the latest season as he reached 2,500 winners on the Flat in Britain when the two-year-old Legend of Xanadu struck in a listed contest at Doncaster in October. However, the former England international footballer—who first started training in 1989 and enjoyed notable success with the likes of Queen's Logic, Youmzain and Zafeen among others—then surprised everyone when he announced just a few days later that he would be handing over the licence to son Jack at the end of the year.

Jack Channon has reportedly started his training career with around 60 horses in his care at West Ilsley, including two of our *Fifty* with Rathgar now joining Ingra Tor on the list, both horses owned by Jon and Julia Aisbitt, huge supporters of the Channon stable over the years. Rathgar rounded off a most promising two-year-old campaign with success in a novice event at Goodwood in October, leading under pressure two furlongs out and keeping going well from there to win by two and a half lengths. That victory came on the back of two promising efforts at the same venue and, all the while, he gave the distinct impression there'll be even better to come from him when he's faced with a stiffer test of stamina as a three-year-old.

Indeed, the key feature of virtually all of Rathgar's runs so far has been his strength at the finish, clearly taking more after his sire Ulysses, a top-class performer over middle-distances, than his dam Why We Dream, a dual winner at around a mile and a half-sister to the smart Johan, winner of last year's Lincoln for these connections. With the frame to keep on improving for a while longer yet, Rathgar strongly appeals as the type to excel in middle-distance handicaps in 2023 when an opening BHA mark of 83 could prove very lenient. **Jack Channon**

Conclusion: *Strong at the finish on all three starts at two and appeals as the type to thrive over middle-distances as a three-year-old; likely to stay 1½m*

Remarquee   95P

3 b.f. Kingman – Regardez (Champs Elysees)
2022 7g* Sep 29

Ralph Beckett enjoyed another fine campaign in 2022 with Kinross, Lezoo, Prosperous Voyage and Westover all winning Group 1 races. Lezoo was the pick of the two-year-olds, but the yard's overall exploits in that division were impressive, their total of 11 debut winners during the Flat season bettered by only five other stables in Britain or Ireland. Beckett's prowess with two-year-old debutants was never more evident than on a Thursday at Salisbury in late-September when he sent out successful newcomers in the first three races on the card. His first two winners that afternoon, Bluestocking and If Not Now, are both names to note for the season ahead, but for our money the third one, Remarquee, might well prove the pick of the bunch.

One of just three fillies in a field made up mostly of colts and geldings, Remarquee did extremely well to make a winning start over seven furlongs, briefly showing signs of greenness when shaken up before quickening smartly to run down the odds-on favourite in the final 50 yards. She was well on the top at the finish, ultimately winning by a length and a quarter, and it wasn't just a case of style over substance, either. A very useful timefigure highlighted that Remarquee ran to a notably high level of form for a newcomer and was fully deserving of the rarely-awarded Timeform large 'P', denoting the likelihood of significant improvement.

Remarquee is from a fine family her trainer knows very well—Beckett trained her dam and grand-dam, as well as Group 1-winning relatives Scope and Look Here, for owner Julian Richmond-Watson—and she looks another exciting prospect for her yard in 2023. The way she scored on her debut leaves no doubt she'll stay a mile but, as a daughter of Kingman out of a mare who was useful at up to a mile and a quarter, it remains to be seen whether she'll stay so well as some of her illustrious relatives. Whatever her trip requirements prove to be, we're not in much doubt that Remarquee is a really smart filly in the making. ***Ralph Beckett***

Conclusion: *Well-related type whose striking winning debut was backed up by the clock; open to any amount of improvement and looks set to make an impact at pattern level*

Simon Baker (Remarquee): *"There weren't many two-year-old newcomers that excited me more last season than Remarquee, who impressed as much visually as she did on the clock when winning at Salisbury and looks sure to make up into a pattern-class filly in 2023 for a stable that I reckon is set for an excellent year."*

Sea Eagle   90p

3 br.g. Time Test – Vassaria (Ire) (Rock of Gibraltar (Ire))
2022 8g⁴ 7g³ p8s* Oct 22

William Haggas saddled no fewer than 20 winners in three-year-old handicaps run over a mile and a quarter plus in Britain in 2022, a tally surpassed by only Charlie and Mark Johnston (24). It was a similar story in 2021 and it's worth pointing out that, compared to the Johnstons, Haggas had far fewer runners in such races in both years. It follows then that highlighting a horse of this ilk from Somerville Lodge to include in this year's *Fifty* was something we were very keen to do, and Sea Eagle appears to fit the bill perfectly.

Sea Eagle improved with each run in a trio of two-year-old maidens in the latter part of 2022, looking that bit more mature each time, and he opened his account comfortably over a mile at Chelmsford when last seen in October. He was a touch keen held up but impressed with the speed with which he made up ground into the straight before coming away nicely in the final furlong, ultimately winning by three lengths with a good bit of authority. The form is by no means spectacular, but it's his run-to-run progression, together with a sales price that rose significantly each time he went through the ring—he fetched €100,000 as a two-year-old having been sold for just 7,000 guineas as a foal—that marks him out as one likely to go on improving into this year having been gelded during the winter.

Among his sire Time Test's first crop of three-year-olds in 2022 were the Group 3 winner Rocchigiani and two other members of our *Fifty*, the improving Okeechobee and, interestingly in the context of Sea Eagle, La Yakel, also trained by Haggas and successful in a valuable event at Ascot in September when making his handicap debut from a BHA mark of 87. As for Sea Eagle, he's been given an opening mark of 86 and, though not overly lenient on the face of it, it's one that he should be capable of progressing well beyond in time, particularly as he goes up in trip. ***William Haggas***

Conclusion: *Made gradual progress in three starts at two and has the makings of a useful middle-distance handicapper as a three-year-old; will stay 1¼m*

Silver Legend (Ire)   79P

3 gr.c. Dark Angel (Ire) – Propel (Ire) (Dubawi (Ire))
2022 6m⁴ Aug 7

The Sky Bet Sunday Series has been a very welcome addition to the Flat calendar over the last two summers, providing plentiful good prize-money opportunities for horses who would ordinarily be competing for less (generally resulting in sizeable, competitive fields) and also potentially exposing racing to a new audience by virtue of its late-Sunday afternoon slot on ITV.

It was at one of these meetings—at Haydock in August—that Silver Legend made his debut in a valuable six-furlong maiden. He shaped with conspicuous promise in finishing fourth (beaten three and a half lengths) behind the subsequent French Group 2 winner Charyn, finishing with a flourish having missed the break and run green in rear (also jumped a path early). It's also worth noting that his high draw was almost certainly a disadvantage as the three who finished ahead of him all raced more towards the far side of the track. It was an initial effort that screamed 'abundant improvement likely' and, though Silver Legend wasn't seen again, that shouldn't be taken as a negative given his trainer's generally patient approach.

Ascertaining what Silver Legend's optimum trip could be is no easy task at this stage, especially given Dark Angel's ability to sire winners over all sorts of distances, but it's safe to assume that he'll be suited by further than six furlongs—his dam is an unraced half-sister to the very smart winner at up to a mile and a half Royal Bench. **William Haggas**

Conclusion: *Eye-catching debut strongly suggests that significantly better can be expected when he's next seen, a maiden success likely to be a formality before being asked to tackle stronger opposition; will be suited by at least 7f*

Slipofthepen   97P

3 ch.c. Night of Thunder (Ire) – Free Verse (Danehill Dancer (Ire))
2022 p8s* Nov 30

One of The Queen's very best horses Aureole—the 1953 Derby runner-up who won the Coronation Cup and King George VI and Queen Elizabeth Stakes as a four-year-old—was also one of the first winners she owned during her close and lengthy association with racing. The signs are that The King has also found a very good horse early in his monarchy as Slipofthepen, who carried the royal colours to success at Kempton just months into the reign of King Charles III, scored in such impressive style on debut to suggest he, like Aureole, could be competing at the highest level.

Presumably a late developer, Slipofthepen didn't make his first appearance on a racecourse until the end of November, but plenty was clearly expected of him as he was sent off the 6/5-on favourite in a novice event over a mile. The only anxious moment for his supporters came when he showed his inexperience at the start (awkward leaving the stalls), but he hardly put a foot wrong besides that, making rapid headway against the rail early in the straight and just needing to be nudged out from there as he forged clear in the final furlong to win by five and a half lengths.

Admittedly, Slipofthepen beat no more than a fair bunch at Kempton, but it was still encouraging that he managed to show so much speed given the stamina on the dam's side of his pedigree. The pick of his siblings is Frontispiece, who was successful at up to 13 furlongs, while Quadrille, a smart performer at up to a mile and a quarter, is a generation back in the family tree, so his future most likely lies at middle-distances as a three-year-old. A Derby trial looks a logical starting point in the spring and, who knows, perhaps Slipofthepen can go one better than Aureole and become the first royal winner of the blue riband at Epsom in well over a century. ***John & Thady Gosden***

Conclusion: *Created a hugely favourable impression on his sole start at two and looks to have the potential to take high rank among the classic generation at middle-distances*

 # Spanish (Ire)   97p
4 ch.f. Lope de Vega (Ire) – Czabo (Sixties Icon)
2022 7m^3 8g^4 10m^5 p8s* 8.3g* Sep 26

Connections have had to be patient with Spanish—a well-bred, lengthy, rather unfurnished filly—but she was very much going the right way towards the end of the latest campaign and can hopefully pick up where she left off. Spanish failed to make it to the course as a juvenile and her inexperience was evident during her first few outings last term, but the penny seemed to drop at Kempton on her fourth start as she picked up powerfully to brush aside a rival with some fairly useful form in the book.

Spanish was impressively strong at the finish at Kempton and it was a similar story next time on her handicap debut at Hamilton where she looked in a bit of trouble over a furlong out but kept on well up the rising ground to hit the front close home and score by a neck. A steady gallop masked Spanish's superiority at Hamilton and a true tempo promises to bring about a bigger performance from this progressive filly.

Spanish has only raced on good or faster ground on turf—she's clearly effective on polytrack based on what she showed at Kempton—but it will be interesting to see how she fares when encountering some cut as her dam, Czabo, won a Group 3 over a mile on heavy going. Spanish is the second foal out of Czabo and a half-sister to Coill Avon (by Kingman), who showed useful form during his short career and claimed the notable scalp of St Mark's Basilica when winning his maiden at the Curragh. Coill Avon was unraced beyond six furlongs but, like their dam, Spanish has already shown she stays a mile well. ***William Haggas***

Conclusion: *Well-bred filly who progressed sharply towards the end of last season, impressing with how powerfully she finished off her races; is in excellent hands and can carry on improving*

Tafreej (Ire) 88p

3 b.g. Shamardal (USA) – Taqaareed (Ire) (Sea The Stars (Ire))
2022 6m⁶ 6g³ 6d* Oct 10

No trainer has more entries in our *Fifty* than William Haggas and Tafreej is the last of six horses from Somerville Lodge who we think it could pay to keep on the right side in 2023. Successful on the last of his three starts as a two-year-old, Tafreej remains with plenty of untapped potential and there should be more to come from him as he gains in experience.

Tafreej left his debut form well behind when finishing third in a six-furlong maiden at Newbury in September, keeping on well to be beaten just a length and a quarter, and he then made the most of a good opportunity to get off the mark in a novice event over the same distance at Yarmouth a few weeks later. Admittedly, he barely needed to improve to justify short odds on the last occasion, but there was still plenty to like about the manner in which he got the job done, travelling smoothly and quickly asserting to win by two and a quarter lengths having been produced to lead over a furlong out. The frame was filled by a pair of once-raced improvers and a promising newcomer, while a good timefigure also adds substance to the form.

There is plenty of stamina on the distaff side of Tafreej's pedigree—his dam is a sister to the Oaks winner Taghrooda—though his half-brother, Ubahha (by Dubawi), registered his sole career win to date over five furlongs. For his part, Tafreej promises to be suited by at least seven furlongs, but the way he travelled through his races at two suggests his connections don't need to be in any rush to step him up in trip. He'll start life in handicaps from a BHA mark of 84, which looks workable, and it will be no surprise if he's targeted at some of those valuable six-furlong events restricted to his age group in the first part of the season. ***William Haggas***

Conclusion: *Confirmed the promise of his second start when opening his account at Yarmouth and has the tools to develop into a useful three-year-old; blessed with plenty of speed but will be suited by 7f+ when the time comes*

Tarjeeh (Ire) 103p

3 b.c. Churchill (Ire) – Myturn (Ire) (Rock of Gibraltar (Ire))
2022 6.1m⁴ 7g* Jul 15

The expectation was that 2022 would be a quieter year for Owen Burrows and his team due to the downsizing of the Shadwell operation after the death of its founder Sheikh Hamdan Al Maktoum. In many ways, it was. The name Owen Burrows—who had previously trained in a private capacity for Sheikh Hamdan—was certainly a less common sight in racecards and he saddled only 67 runners on the Flat in Britain in 2022, down from a high of 182 in 2018.

However, it was what those 67 runners did that really counted and, amazingly given everything that came before it, the latest season was in many ways the best of Burrows' training career to date. It was comfortably his best by total prize money won (£956,200) and so too by strike rate (31%) having saddled 21 winners from those 67 runners. Crucially, Burrows also made a deserved breakthrough in Group 1 company with the high-class older horses Hukum (Coronation Cup) and Minzaal (Haydock Sprint Cup), while Alflaila and Anmaat both achieved a similar level of form when winning in lesser pattern company.

All bar Minzaal are set to return in 2023 and it could be another exciting year for Burrows, who also has a couple of promising three-year-olds in his care, perhaps none more so than Tarjeeh. Given a considerate introduction on his debut at Windsor in June, finishing a never-nearer fourth under a hands-and-heels ride, Tarjeeh was much improved with that run under his belt when getting off the mark at Newbury the following month, clearly relishing the step up to seven furlongs as he ran on well to win by half a length. The timefigure suggests he was full value for a useful performance and five of the next seven home have won races subsequently, while the runner-up Dancing Magic, who ended the campaign still a maiden after five starts, showed useful form when finishing a close-up fourth in the Group 3 Autumn Stakes at Newmarket.

A well-made colt, Tarjeeh was bought for 40,000 guineas as a foal and then cost exactly four times as much when being sold again as a yearling. His sire Churchill was responsible for Timeform's highest-rated three-year-old in Europe in 2022, the Prix du Jockey Club/ Eclipse winner Vadeni, while his unraced dam is closely related to Temida, a Group 1 winner over a mile and a half in Germany. Of his two siblings to have raced so far, Muay Thai (by Acclamation) was a winner over seven furlongs in Britain and Australia Cape (by Australia) was a winner at up to 11 furlongs in Spain. For his part, Tarjeeh seems sure to stay at least a mile and has the makings of a smart colt having been given plenty of time since his two runs last summer. ***Owen Burrows***

Conclusion: *Impressed in his appearance and with the way he stayed on to win a deep novice event on his second start at Newbury; will stay 1m and looks a potential pattern performer*

Torito   81P
3 b.c. Kingman – Montare (Ire) (Montjeu (Ire))
2022 8v³ Oct 21

American owner-breeder George Strawbridge has had plenty of success with the fillies in Torito's immediate family but, if his very promising debut is anything to go by, Torito looks like proving an above-average colt in the well-known white and green

Torito is a half-brother to Park Hill Stakes winner Mimikyu

colours. His dam Montare was a smart racemare herself for Jonathan Pease in France, though she had some of the typical quirks associated with daughters of Montjeu, having a tendency to carry her head awkwardly, hang and sometimes flash her tail. But that didn't stop her winning seven races, with her biggest success coming as a four-year-old in the Group 1 Prix Royal-Oak over just short of two miles.

With her racing days over, Montare has been a terrific broodmare for Strawbridge, with the best of her daughters being Journey, she too a Group 1 winner in the Fillies' And Mares' Stakes at Ascot. Journey is now a successful broodmare herself, being the dam of Inner Space, a potential Oaks filly for Torito's connections after an impressive winning debut at Kempton last year. More recently, Montare has produced smart sisters to Journey in Indigo Girl, winner of the May Hill Stakes and runner-up in the Fillies' Mile in 2020, and last season's Park Hill Stakes winner Mimikyu.

Like Journey and Mimikyu, Torito had just the one run at two, showing more ability than either of those two did at that age. He was clearly expected to show plenty on his debut, too, as he was sent off the 11/8 favourite in a field of 14 for a novice at Newbury in October. In the end, he found a couple with prior experience too strong, but there was a lot to like about his third place behind It's All About You and Goodfella, beaten a head and three quarters of a length. Travelling well just behind the pace, Torito was shaken up to join the leaders a furlong out but ran green and couldn't quicken, with Frankie Dettori not subjecting him to a hard race in the testing conditions once his chance had gone. Torito seems sure to have learned plenty from that experience and is bound to progress for greater tests of stamina at three. Although Torito is by miler Kingman, his half-brother Travelling Man was a smart stayer in France despite being by sprinter Oasis Dream. ***John & Thady Gosden***

Conclusion: *Shaped with plenty of promise when third at Newbury on his sole two-year-old start and, with his dam and a half-sister both Group 1 winners, is bred to come into his own over middle-distances this year*

Vee Sight 94p

4 b.g. Churchill (Ire) – Look So (Efisio)
2022 9m* 9.9m⁴ 9.9g³ 10g⁶ Sep 16

After making a successful handicap debut on his reappearance at Sandown in June last year, Vee Sight then failed to add to his tally in three subsequent starts, though that doesn't tell the whole story as he shaped with abundant promise on more than one occasion. Yet to race beyond a mile and a quarter, he often left the impression that he's crying out for further and, if longer trips can eke out a bit more improvement, then he's certainly on a good mark for a stable which enjoyed its most lucrative campaign to date in 2022.

On his penultimate start back at Sandown in August, Vee Sight finished third in a really competitive handicap, sticking to his task well to be beaten only four and a quarter lengths behind a pair of in-form and progressive rivals. He was then sent off the 2/1 favourite when dropped down in grade for a 19-runner handicap at Newbury in September and, though finishing only sixth, it's perhaps worth putting a line through that run as he wasn't seen to anything like best effect. In fact, he did very well under the circumstances to pass the post only two and a quarter lengths behind the winner having met plenty of trouble in the final three furlongs, finishing with running left and looking unlucky not to go a bit closer.

Ralph Beckett is no stranger to a patient approach and Vee Sight is still unexposed having had just seven starts to date. Closely related to Scope (by Teofilo), who won the Group 1 Prix Royal-Oak over nearly two miles, Vee Sight is from a family who typically improve with age, and both his pedigree and the way he shaped when last seen suggest a step up to a mile and a half could be the key to unlocking further progress. He already has some useful form to his name and a solid base to build from with a BHA mark of 84 heading into his four-year-old campaign. ***Ralph Beckett***

Vee Sight remains with potential as a four-year-old

Conclusion: *Didn't enjoy the rub of the green on his final start of last season and should have more to offer as his stamina is drawn out further as a four-year-old; likely to stay at least 1½m*

Willem Twee   108

4 b.g. Ribchester (Ire) – Paulinie (Royal Applause)
2022 p7s⁴ t7.1s² 6m* 6f* p6s* 6g p6s² Oct 5

It's not clear whether Willem Twee is named after the nineteenth-century King of the Netherlands or the Eerste Divisie football club that shares his moniker, but either one gives a good clue as to the origins of his owner Chris Van Hoorn. Van Hoorn's silks—combining the oranje of the Dutch national team with half-white sleeves—have been carried by some smart performers on British racecourses over the last 30 years or so, and we're optimistic that Willem Twee can progress to that kind of level himself by the end of 2023, hopefully winning some good sprint handicaps along the way.

As a son of the high-class miler Ribchester, it was little surprise that Willem Twee started out over seven furlongs, and he showed plenty of ability to hit the frame over that trip on his first two starts on the all-weather, but it was when he was dropped back to six furlongs that his form really took off. He was a comfortable winner of a maiden at Doncaster in June and then made an opening BHA mark of 78 look wholly inadequate in a handicap over the same course and distance the following month. He was also first past the post on his next outing at Kempton in August, crossing the line with an advantage of two and three-quarter lengths with plenty in hand, though he was later disqualified after testing positive for an anti-inflammatory medication that can be used with veterinary prescription but is prohibited from being present in a horse's body on raceday.

Still, it's worth noting that the form of that race at Kempton—which was run in a fast time—has worked out really well, with the horses in behind Willem Twee combining to win eight races before the end of 2022. Admittedly, Willem Twee ended his year with a couple of defeats, though a quickish turnaround can excuse his below-par effort in a handicap at Ascot in September, and he got back on track when last seen filling the runner-up spot in a conditions event at Kempton in October, doing well to be beaten just a length and a quarter having conceded first run to the winner.

Willem Twee will start the new season from a BHA mark of 95, which will get him into some good-quality sprint handicaps, and he's very much the type to improve again and make his mark in such company, his strong-travelling style making him an ideal sort for big-field sprints. He has been gelded over the winter and, a fluent mover, has produced his best form so far on top of the ground and on polytrack. *James Fanshawe*

Conclusion: *Strong-travelling sort who remains lightly-raced and looks tailormade for some of the big sprint handicaps in the Flat racing calendar*

Yorkshire (Ire)   85p
3 b.c. Harry Angel (Ire) – Totsiyah (Ire) (Dalakhani (Ire))
2022 6m³ 6d* Oct 14

Readers with long memories might remember another Yorkshire, a smart stayer who began his career with Paul Cole in the late 1990s in the all-green colours of Fahd Salman. Sired by Salman's Derby winner Generous and out of a sister to another of his best horses, Oaks winner Ramruma, Yorkshire didn't live up to his classic breeding, but among his better efforts were finishing second in the Queen Alexandra Stakes and being beaten little more than a length when fifth in the Melbourne Cup. Switched to jumps for Dai Williams later in his career, Yorkshire won his first five races over hurdles in early-season novice events under Richard Johnson, hacking up under the burden of 12-9 in the last of them!

The latest horse to bear the name of the county "where everything's done proper" according to the tea advert is an altogether speedier type and has a much closer association with Yorkshire as he's trained at Coverham near Middleham by Ed Bethell, who took over the licence at Thorngill Stables from his father James at the beginning of 2021. Yorkshire carries the black and white colours of Clarendon Thoroughbred Racing whose syndicates were founded in 1997 by Bethell's parents. Many of the Clarendon horses have carried the names of Yorkshire villages, including Fearby, Ed Bethell's first listed winner, but the fact that Yorkshire, a breeze-up purchase who cost 100,000 guineas, has been named after the whole county might be an indication he's held in some regard.

Yorkshire certainly made a promising start to his career in two starts last season. He made his debut over six furlongs at Haydock in August, in a valuable maiden restricted to newcomers at one of the Sky Bet Sunday Series meetings, and shaped well in running on for third, a length and a half behind Charyn, later a Group 2 winner in France in the Criterium de Maisons-Laffitte. That made Yorkshire the one to beat in a novice at Redcar in October and, under softer conditions than for his debut, he was well on top at the finish in justifying short odds by two and a quarter lengths from Colnago. By the top-class sprinter Harry Angel, Yorkshire comes from a very successful family, with his grandam being a half-sister to the 2000 Guineas winner Footstepsinthesand to name just one. *Edward Bethell*

Conclusion: *Cost plenty at the breeze-ups and confirmed debut promise when off the mark at the second attempt at Redcar, so looks a useful handicapper in the making*

SECTION

2

Alexandroupolis (Ire)   96p

3 b.c. Camelot – Jazz Cat (Ire) (Tamayuz)
2022 8.6s* Sep 6

Aidan O'Brien has the firm favourite for the Derby with Auguste Rodin, who has a Group 1 win to his name already thanks to his comfortable victory in the Futurity Trophy. But Ireland's champion trainer rarely goes to Epsom single-handed and Alexandroupolis looks just the type to join his stablemate in the Derby field with a big showing in the classic trials. O'Brien has dominated the maiden for two-year-olds over an extended mile at Galway's September meeting in the last decade or so and Alexandroupolis became the stable's ninth winner of that race since 2011. Its recent winners include the likes of Irish Derby winner Sovereign and top-class stayer Kyprios, while it was also the race in which Ballydoyle's shock 2020 Derby winner Serpentine made a more discreet debut, beating only one home.

Given Aidan O'Brien's record in the race, it was somewhat surprising that his two runners in last year's contest, both of them newcomers, were allowed to start at 17/2, but that was due to Joseph O'Brien fielding Magnetar, who was a short-priced favourite after showing plenty of ability on both his starts. Despite being easy to back, Alexandroupolis ran out a ready winner once Wayne Lordan obtained a clear run. Going well but in need of a gap entering the straight, Alexandroupolis quickened to lead inside the final furlong once getting daylight and came home a length and three-quarters ahead of slow-starting stablemate Espionage, who finished well from even further back. While Alexandroupolis wasn't seen out again, Espionage paid him a big compliment by winning a Curragh maiden in emphatic fashion later in the month and then going down by a head in the Criterium International at Saint-Cloud.

While Alexandroupolis's dam Jazz Cat, who was just a modest maiden, ran only at seven furlongs and has produced a winning sprinter by Starspangledbanner, Alexandroupolis, a 240,000 guineas yearling by Camelot, is much more of a staying type. In fact, he could just as well make into a St Leger type as a Derby prospect as his dam's half-sister Kew Gardens won the Doncaster classic in 2018. Kew Gardens' brother Wordsworth was a smart stayer for Ballydoyle last year and was runner-up earlier in his career in the Queen's Vase and Grand Prix de Paris (both races which Kew Gardens won) as well as third in the Irish Derby. ***Aidan O'Brien***

Conclusion: *Readily beat a stablemate who later went close at Group 1 level on his only start at two and, related to one of his stable's St Leger winners, is one to look out for in a Derby trial*

Boy Scout 86

3 b.c. Frankel – Qushchi (Encosta de Lago (Aus))
2022 7g^5 7.4d^4 7.1g^2 Sep 20

In another star-studded crop of two-year-olds at Ballydoyle in 2022 that included champion Little Big Bear and Auguste Rodin, Blackbeard, Meditate and Victoria Road, all of whom also struck at the top level, Boy Scout was well down the pecking order. Not all the stable's youngsters are bred to shine in their first season, though, and Boy Scout looks just the type to take much higher rank over longer distances as a three-year-old.

Boy Scout made his debut at the Curragh in early-August when Ryan Moore's pick from two newcomers from Ballydoyle. In a maiden where Joseph O'Brien's Al Riffa was sent off a hot favourite on the way to winning the National Stakes on his next start, it was Aidan O'Brien's other colt Salt Lake City who fared the better of his pair in keeping on well for second. Boy Scout seemed to need the experience more but kept on from well off the pace without being given too hard a race to finish fifth. Boy Scout duly improved in his two remaining starts and shaped similarly in both, going in snatches but ultimately finishing off both races well. Turned out just nine days after his debut, at Roscommon, Boy Scout was easy to back and still very much in need of the experience, but he was seemingly getting the hang of things late on as he kept on well to finish fourth to Spirit Genie. His final outing came at Listowel in September where he came up against another odds-on shot in Tiverton for Dermot Weld and again did his best work at the finish to go down by half a length.

Boy Scout, who was tongue tied for all his starts, raced only at seven furlongs at two but will be well suited by at least a mile and a quarter this season. Even by Frankel's standards he was an expensive yearling purchase at 925,000 guineas. From the family of the Dewhurst Stakes and St James's Palace Stakes winner Grand Lodge, Boy Scout's dam Qushchi was a useful middle-distance filly whose wins included a couple of mile-and-a-half handicaps at three. She's already produced two smart winners in Mrs Sippy, a Grade 2 winner in the US over 11 furlongs, and Phantom Flight, an impressive winner of a handicap over a mile and a quarter at last year's Ebor Festival. *Aidan O'Brien*

Conclusion: *Expensive yearling purchase who was too immature to get his head in front at two but progressed with each run; looks the type to take off over middle-distances in 2023*

Bua (Ire)   98p

4 b.f. Dark Angel (Ire) – Clem Fandango (Fr) (Elzaam (Aus))
2022 p6s⁶ 7v* Oct 23

County Tipperary trainer Paddy Twomey enjoyed much his best campaign yet in 2022 with 32 wins on Irish soil at an excellent strike rate of 30%. Among those wins were his first Group 1 successes thanks to La Petite Coco in the Pretty Polly Stakes and Pearls Galore who went one better than the year before when winning the Matron Stakes. Another success story among the stable's four-year-old fillies was Rosscarbery, who started the year as a maiden from another yard but promptly won five of her first six starts for her new stable and went close to becoming another Group 1 winner when beaten a neck in the Prix Jean Romanet at Deauville.

Both La Petite Coco and Rosscarberry fetched a million guineas when sent to the sales at the end of the year, but Twomey could have another smart four-year-old filly on his hands this season if Bua continues to go the right way. He's had to be patient with her, though, because while Twomey said he thought she was his best two-year-old, an injury and then "a few little hiccups" meant that it was the autumn of her three-year-old season before she made it to the track. When she finally did make her debut at Dundalk in October, the well-backed Bua was too green to do herself justice, making late headway into sixth after a slow start.

Bua clearly learnt plenty from that experience, though, because she was a different proposition when fitted with a visor at the Curragh just nine days later. Conditions were heavy and Bua was just about the only one to handle them as she travelled well before improving to lead over a furlong out. She drew right away from there to coast home by 12 lengths from the favourite Lizzy's Filly, with the remainder finishing well strung out. Whilst not the easiest race to assess, the runner-up had some fairly useful form to her name, while Bua's timefigure was a useful one. Bua clearly stays at least seven furlongs in testing conditions, but even that's a bit further than she might be expected to get on breeding as she's by Dark Angel out of Clem Fandango, who was a useful five-furlong performer, winning a listed race at Ayr at two when she was also placed in the Queen Mary Stakes and Cornwallis Stakes. *Paddy Twomey*

Conclusion: *Evidently well regarded by her up-and-coming trainer and showed why when hacking up in heavy ground on her second start after a belated debut in the autumn; sure to progress and win more races*

Espionage (Ire)   110p

3 b.c. Galileo (Ire) – Even Song (Ire) (Mastercraftsman (Ire))
2022 8.6s² 7s* 8v² Oct 22

British and Irish horses made a splash in several races at Saint-Cloud at the backend of the 2022 season, especially in the Criterium International where the trio of raiders filled the first three places. Donnacha O'Brien's Proud And Regal showed a likeable attitude to go one better than when chasing home Al Riffa in the National Stakes at the Curragh the time before, but perhaps the horse to take out of the race was the runner-up, Espionage, who lacked the winner's experience but showed much improved form in going down only narrowly.

Stepping up markedly in grade having contested mere maidens at Galway and the Curragh in two previous starts, Espionage was sent straight to the front in the Criterium International and, as usual when the ground is testing at Saint-Cloud, he brought the field over to the stand side in the straight. He was ridden soon after and fought off a couple of challengers on his outer before being tackled by the eventual winner in the final furlong, ultimately losing out by a head having stuck to his task in determined fashion.

Espionage sheds his maiden tag at the Curragh

Even as a juvenile, the one-mile trip in France seemed a bare minimum for Espionage, so it was to his credit that he won his maiden over seven furlongs at the Curragh in September, that success coming after he'd shaped well when filling the runner-up spot over an extended mile at Galway earlier in the month. He confirmed that promise in emphatic fashion when making all by a length and three-quarters on his second start, quickly having matters in hand after moving into a clear lead entering the final furlong, and the timefigure highlighted that he was full value for a useful performance.

Espionage is bred to come into his own over middle-distances—he is by the late Galileo and out of the Ribblesdale Stakes winner Even Song, herself a half-sister to the St Leger winner Simple Verse—and it's highly unlikely that we've seen the best of him just yet with that in mind. Already smart, the next step in his development will probably involve a Derby trial in the spring and Epsom could well beckon if he builds on his brief but productive two-year-old campaign in the way that we're expecting. **Aidan O'Brien**

Conclusion: *Came a long way in a short space of time at two and very much the type to go on improving as a three-year-old; will stay at least 1¼m*

 # Express Way (Ire) 80p
4 b.f. Dark Angel (Ire) – Alluring Park (Ire) (Green Desert (USA))
2022 p10.7s* Nov 11

Blistering trade in the sales ring last autumn saw a host of records tumble, but one benchmark which remained untouched was the highest price paid for a yearling in Europe. That figure remains the 5 million guineas paid for Al Naamah—a daughter of Galileo out of Alluring Park—at Book 1 of the Tattersalls October Yearling Sale in 2013.

The success of Al Naamah's sister, Was, in the Oaks at Epsom the previous year undoubtedly contributed to such a remarkable fee, while Alluring Park herself boasts an exceptional pedigree being a daughter of Phoenix Champion Stakes winner Park Express and a half-sister to Derby winner New Approach. Al Naamah may not have lived up to her sales price, but she was still a useful sort who gained valuable black-type when runner-up in the Group 3 Prix Cleopatre and in a listed contest at Longchamp. Al Naamah is one of five of Alluring Park's offspring who have achieved a Timeform rating of 100 or above, and it is hoped there will be at least one more on that list by the end of the year as Express Way looked like a useful prospect when making a successful debut at Dundalk in November.

Connections have had to be patient with Express Way, who didn't appear on a racecourse in public until seven weeks shy of her fourth birthday, but she made a highly encouraging start to her career, overcoming signs of inexperience (and market weakness) to win by half a length. A steady gallop in that maiden—staged over just shy of 11 furlongs—meant that they finished in a bit of a heap and the form is nothing flash, but Express Way can take a big step forward with that outing under her belt and ought to be placed to good effect by the excellent Paddy Twomey, with connections presumably keen to secure some black-type given her valuable pedigree. **Paddy Twomey**

Conclusion: *Well-bred mare who made a successful start to her career; should improve for that experience and one to note for a trainer who has created a big impression in recent seasons*

Gambe Veloci (Ire) 82

4 gr.g. Caravaggio (USA) – Neutral (Beat Hollow)
2022 8g² 8d² 7.1g³ Sep 20

Gambe Veloci translates from Italian as 'fast legs', but the grey didn't get a fair chance to live up to his name when a beaten odds-on favourite at Listowel in September as his race was effectively ended by interference on the home turn. Gambe Veloci, the 9/4-on favourite, attempted to make headway up the inside turning in, but he found himself caught on the heels of a struggling rival and, by the time he was switched a furlong out, the first two had gone beyond recall and he had to settle for a never-threatening third. It would be unfair to judge Gambe Veloci on that performance, given how the race developed, and his two previous efforts give a better indication of his ability.

On his debut at Leopardstown in August, Gambe Veloci was very slowly away and showed further signs of inexperience when asked for his effort, initially looking green under pressure, but he stayed on strongly inside the final furlong to fill the runner-up spot, beaten a length and three-quarters. He then shaped similarly on his next start at Cork, clearly still learning—a fact he betrayed when hanging right in the straight—but once again making significant late headway to grab second, beaten just half a length this time and arguably deserving extra credit given where he came from.

A combination of greenness and bad luck in running prevented Gambe Veloci from showing the full extent of his ability as a three-year-old, but he's been handed an opening handicap mark of just 73 and that looks lenient, particularly as he retains the potential to progress. **Joseph O'Brien**

Conclusion: *Showed promise when runner-up in a couple of 1m maidens and his latest defeat can be overlooked after getting no luck in running; has been handed a lenient opening mark*

Maxine (Ire)   78

5 b.m. Maxios – Saltita (Ire) (Galileo (Ire))
2022 10.2g p12s⁶ 10m 12.2s⁶ 16.6s⁶ 10.9d Oct 23

Emmet Mullins has created a huge impression in a relatively short space of time since taking out his trainer's licence, memorably sending out Noble Yeats last year to become the first seven-year-old winner of the Grand National since Bogskar in 1940. Noble Yeats carried the silks of Robert Waley-Cohen on that famous afternoon at Aintree, but he had started his career running in the colours of Paul Byrne, an owner who has enjoyed notable success with Mullins, including with The Shunter, who bagged a £100,000 bonus for following up his win in the 2021 Morebattle Hurdle at Kelso with victory in the Plate at that season's Cheltenham Festival.

Byrne—whose jumps winners include So Scottish and Filey Bay who, like The Shunter, have been bought by J. P. McManus—has had only a handful of runners on the Flat, but he has an interesting one for the upcoming season in Maxine. Maxine failed to beat a rival on her last couple of starts for Harry Dunlop, but she offered a lot more encouragement when sixth on her first outing for Byrne and Mullins in an apprentice handicap run over a mile and a half at Galway in September, catching the eye as the only runner to make any meaningful progress from rear, doing so despite being short of room when going well on the turn for home. Maxine also shaped with promise on her next outing at the Curragh in October, staying on steadily to finish sixth in a valuable and competitive handicap over half a mile further, despite things again not going ideally (she stumbled on the home turn). She was flying too high when having a crack at a Group 3 in Germany on her final outing of the campaign, but a mark of 68 looks well within her grasp and one her astute connections can exploit.
Emmet Mullins

Conclusion: *Lost her way for her previous yard but has made an encouraging start for new connections and looks set to take advantage of a falling mark; versatile with regards trip*

Sea Gardens (Fr)   82p

3 ch.c. Siyouni (Fr) – Bal de La Rose (Ire) (Cadeaux Genereux)
2022 8s⁴ Oct 15

Leopardstown backend maidens tend to be a consistent source of winners and the contest won by Peking Opera in mid-October is already proving a perfect case in point. However, it's not the winner who appears in our *Fifty*, but the highly promising Sea Gardens instead.

Sea Gardens very much caught the eye when finishing fourth in the aforementioned maiden run over a mile at Leopardstown, a race for which he was sent off the 9/2 third choice of punters. He duly produced a promising first effort, his inexperience very evident after he'd done well to get himself into a position to challenge following a slow start. He was beaten just a length and a quarter at the line and his performance was arguably worth marking up given the greenness he showed and the fact that two of the three who finished ahead of him had the benefit of previous experience. The exception was another newcomer in second, Aidan O'Brien's Bertinelli, who was one of the first to advertise the strength of that form when going one place better on his next start at Dundalk. He isn't alone, either, as the fifth, sixth and ninth also won next time, adding substance to the visual impression made by Sea Gardens.

By Siyouni and a half-brother to the smart Danceteria, who won a Group 1 over a mile and a quarter in Germany, Sea Gardens certainly has plenty to recommend him on pedigree and he clearly looks the part as well having cost his connections 170,000 guineas as a yearling. He showed more than enough on his debut to suggest he possesses his fair share of ability, too, and there should be lots more to come from him as he gains in experience as a three-year-old. *Joseph O'Brien*

Conclusion: *Shaped well amidst greenness on his sole start at two and looks banker material for a maiden before testing the waters in better company in 2023*

 # Tahiyra (Ire) 116P

3 b.f. Siyouni (Fr) – Tarana (Ire) (Cape Cross (Ire))
2022 7d* 7v* Sep 11

Dermot Weld invariably has a runner in the seven-furlong maiden for two-year-old fillies at the Galway Festival and she often turns out to be a good one. For example, in 2016 he won it with another Aga Khan filly, the smart Eziyra, whose later wins included the Blandford Stakes, while Tahirya's half-sister Tarnawa was third on her debut in 2018. Aidan O'Brien has targeted some good fillies at the same race, too, and had the odds-on favourite for the latest edition with Dower House, a sister to Churchill. However, Weld's Tahiyra readily brushed her aside with a striking turn of foot and quickened away to win by five and a half lengths.

O'Brien's Meditate, unbeaten in four starts, including the Albany Stakes at Royal Ascot, looked like being a much tougher nut for Tahiyra to crack in the Moyglare Stud Stakes at the Curragh nearly seven weeks later, but Tahiyra again left a Ballydoyle favourite in her wake as she took the big step up in class in her stride. Making smooth headway from mid-division and then quickening to lead in the final furlong without Chris Hayes having to go for his whip, Tahiyra was value for more than the two and a quarter lengths she had to spare at the line over Meditate, who in turn pulled well clear of the rest in testing conditions. Tahiyra's time was quicker than the colts managed in the

Tahiyra runs out an impressive winner of the Moyglare Stud Stakes

National Stakes and the form got a big tick when the runner-up went on to win the Breeders' Cup Juvenile Fillies' Turf.

It's unusual for a filly rated as highly as Tahiyra to have Timeform's large 'P' symbol still attached to her rating. But as the impressive winner of both her starts she remains open to above-average improvement and, on form and potential at least, looks a worthy favourite for the 1000 Guineas. She has already achieved a lot more at two than the aforementioned Tarnawa (by Shamardal), a later developer whose form only really took off late in her four-year-old season. Unbeaten in that campaign, she ended 2020 winning the Breeders' Cup Turf and was only beaten three quarters of a length at five in both the Irish Champion Stakes and Prix de l'Arc de Triomphe. That's a further reason to be excited by Tahiyra's prospects this year, both at a mile initially and later over longer trips. ***Dermot Weld***

Conclusion: *Half-sister to connections' high-class filly Tarnawa and has similar potential herself having impressively beaten a future Breeders' Cup winner when making it two from two in the Moyglare Stud Stakes*

White Caviar (Fr)   96p

4 b.f. Australia – Curious Mind (Dansili)
2022 12s⁵ 12.3g² 12d* 11.8v* Oct 18

Galileo Chrome started the 2020 campaign as a once-raced maiden but ended it with a classic win under his belt, showing a very willing attitude to land the St Leger on what would prove to be his final start, subsequently retired to stand as a National Hunt stallion.

Unlike her aforementioned brother—though also trained by Joseph O'Brien, who last year announced his intention to scale down his jumping operation to concentrate primarily on the Flat—White Caviar didn't make the racecourse as a two-year-old, but she showed improved form on each of her four outings last season, making it third time lucky in a Listowel maiden in September before exploiting what had appeared a lenient-looking opening mark on handicap debut at Gowran Park the following month. Making her challenge widest of all in the straight and initially meeting some traffic problems as the field migrated towards the near side, White Caviar forged clear late on to win by two and a quarter lengths having hit the front well inside the final furlong.

White Caviar has done all her racing to date at around a mile and a half, with both victories coming on ground softer than good, and she promises to take her form up another notch when tackling longer trips. In fact, it would be no surprise if she develops into a smart staying handicapper granted more of a test of stamina, the type who could even play a part in races such as the Ebor and Irish Cesarewitch, both of which have seen major prize money injections in recent years. **Joseph O'Brien**

Conclusion: *Progressed again when last seen winning at Gowran and promises to go on improving for a while yet, bound to appreciate more of a test when the time comes*

Billy Nash (White Caviar): *"White Caviar achieved plenty, despite looking a work in progress, in a short space of time last year and there should be plenty more to come from her in 2023. A full-sister to St. Leger winner Galileo Chrome, she looks to be crying out for a step up in trip and has the potential to rate much higher than her current official mark of 90. Connections are likely to go in search of some black type given her pedigree, but they will surely also have one eye on valuable staying handicaps such as the Ebor or the Irish Cesarewitch."*

SECTION

TALKING TO THE TRAINERS

To give some pointers for the new season, we asked a number of leading Flat trainers to pick out a star performer, handicapper and dark horse to follow from their respective stables. Read on to find out which names came back...

Charlie Appleby

Wins-Runs in Britain in 2022	**152-488**
Highest-rated horse in training	**Adayar** Timeform Rating 128

Star Performer: Adayar (128): "He had an interrupted season last year. It was a great reappearance at Doncaster and he backed that up with a courageous run on ground that was testing for him in the Champion Stakes. We're very much working back from the Prince of Wales's Stakes and looking at the Gordon Richards Stakes as a starting point."

Handicapper: First Sight (94p): "He has done little wrong to date. He's won his last two starts and has a pedigree which suggests time and a trip will see further improvement. We would like to work back from a Royal Ascot handicap."

Dark Horse: Measured Time (98P): "He won on his only start at Kempton in February. With his pedigree (half-brother to Rebel's Romance), we hope a step up in trip in the future will see continued progress."

Mick Appleby

Wins-Runs in Britain in 2022	**107-882**
Highest-rated horse in training	**Annaf** Timeform Rating 118

Star Performer: Michaela's Boy (98): "He did well as a two-year-old and we're looking forward to his career as a three-year-old. His first run this year will be in France in March in a listed race over five and a half furlongs at Chantilly."

Handicapper: Bond Boy (81): "He is still improving and probably ahead of his mark."

Dark Horse: King of Bavaria (103+): "After he arrived he was gelded and had a break. He ran well in a fast-track qualifier at Lingfield and we're looking forward to having some fun with him through the summer."

Lezoo won four of her five starts as a two-year-old

Ralph Beckett

Wins-Runs in Britain in 2022   **88-565**

Highest-rated horse in training   **Westover** Timeform Rating 126

Star Performer: Lezoo (112): "She has wintered very well and is likely to start in the Nell Gwyn Stakes. She will also have Guineas entries, but it will be no surprise if she reverts to sprinting."

Handicapper: Promoter (87): "He overachieved at two in light of his dam's staying pedigree and has done very well physically over the winter. I think off 90 he will be competitive."

Dark Horse: Lose Yourself (102p): "She did extremely well to be second in the Oh So Sharp Stakes off one start and her pedigree suggests that she should get better with age."

Michael Bell

Wins-Runs in Britain in 2022	**38-330**
Highest-rated horse in training	**Dillian** Timeform Rating 107

Star Performer: Maylandsea (100): "She ran very well to be second in both the Cornwallis Stakes and Queen Mary Stakes. Hopefully she can train on and win a Group race which she deserves to do."

Handicapper: Mindset (85): "He is bred to improve from two to three and is a horse with a good attitude. Hopefully he will make up into a Saturday handicapper."

Dark Horse: Banderas (89p): "He was very unlucky in defeat on debut and is a horse with an exciting pedigree which shows he could well be above average."

Marco Botti

Wins-Runs in Britain in 2022	**51-396**
Highest-rated horse in training	**Ardakan** Timeform Rating 118

Star Performer: Ardakan (118): "He's a horse with lots of quality. He started off for us in Dubai but looks an exciting horse to run in races over a mile and a half plus during the summer. We're excited to see what he can do."

Handicapper: Strategia (72): "A big, scopey horse who showed plenty of signs of immaturity. He has been gelded over the winter and looks progressive."

Dark Horse: Come Musica (73): "He's always looked to want a real trip and the penny is only just beginning to drop. We were encouraged by his third run."

Karl Burke

Wins-Runs in Britain in 2022	**117-783**
Highest-rated horse in training	**El Caballo** Timeform Rating 116

Star Performer: Dramatised (106): "She will be aimed at another Breeders' Cup in the autumn. Hopefully, she will start in the Temple Stakes at Haydock before running in the King's Stand Stakes at Royal Ascot. The Nunthorpe Stakes at York will be high on the agenda, too."

Handicapper: Lethal Levi (106): "He will be aimed at the Wokingham Stakes at Royal Ascot with one prep run."

Dark Horse: Flight Plan (88p): "He should be winning plenty of races this year."

Owen Burrows

Wins-Runs in Britain in 2022	**21-67**
Highest-rated horse in training	**Hukum** Timeform Rating 127

Star Performer: Hukum (127): "A pretty obvious one really! He's been back with me for a couple of months now, he looks great and is moving well. There are no immediate targets, but he'll probably be aimed for more of a mid-season start, with the obvious races through to the end of the year on his radar."

Handicapper: Tarrabb (100): "I actually don't have many to choose from this year! She is a filly I like a lot. She won three for us last year with her best form on good or faster ground. She's done well physically through the winter and has strengthened up plenty. She should still be competitive off her mark of 91."

Hukum (striped cap) gains a first Group 1 win in the Coronation Cup

Dark Horse: Welleef (unraced): "He is an unraced son of Lope de Vega who showed me plenty in his work at the backend of last year. He actually had a couple of entries but picked up a little niggle which stopped us from running him. He showed a bit of speed in his work, so we'll look to start him over possibly six furlongs or more likely seven in the spring."

Henry Candy

Wins-Runs in Britain in 2022	**12-142**
Highest-rated horse in training	**Twilight Calls** Timeform Rating 117

Star Performer: Run To Freedom (114): "He improved towards the end of last season and should be able to contest the top six-furlong races."

Handicapper: Ring of Light (80+): "He improved in the autumn and could still have a pound or two in hand."

Dark Horse: Cape Vincent (unraced): "He is bred to be sharp and is starting to mature now. He could be okay later in the year."

Harry & Roger Charlton

Wins-Runs in Britain in 2022	**52-293**
Highest-rated horse in training	**Sinjaari** Timeform Rating 116

Star Performer: Time Lock (111p): "She didn't race at two and was lightly-raced as a three-year-old, but when she did race her form was rock solid. She travelled extremely well at York in the Galtres Stakes and was slightly unlucky to be caught by Haskoy up the far rail. She has the scope to improve this year and should stay further if needed."

Handicapper: Valsad (94): "He had quite a lot of racing up until July of last year before he had a nice break. He ran well to be third in the valuable handicap at Haydock on his last run and should be progressive from a mark of 85 this year given his breeding."

Dark Horse: Elegancia (70p): "She just had the one run last year in a conditions race at Newbury that we like to run horses in. David Probert gave her a lovely first-time-out ride and taught her plenty. She should stay further than seven furlongs. She is a good-looking filly with a nice pedigree."

Michael Dods

Wins-Runs in Britain in 2022	**57-499**

Highest-rated horse in training	**Commanche Falls** Timeform Rating 119

Star Performer: Azure Blue (106): "She improved throughout 2022 and has wintered well. She should improve again as a four-year-old."

Handicapper: Tatterstall (80): "She was unlucky not to win as a two-year-old and looks sure to improve this year over five or six furlongs."

Dark Horse: Lord Abama (79): "He's joined the yard for this season and looks a horse that will do well over six or seven furlongs."

Charlie Fellowes

Wins-Runs in Britain in 2022	**34-289**

Highest-rated horse in training	**Atrium** Timeform Rating 113

Star Performer: Marbaan (107): "He won the Vintage Stakes impressively before getting stuck in the mud in Ireland and possibly not loving Newmarket in the Dewhurst Stakes. He has done really well over the winter and, being by Oasis Dream, we think he might end up dropping back to sprinting. He will either start in the Greenham Stakes or the Pavilion Stakes."

Handicapper: Atrium (113): "He finished off the year in fine style by winning his last two starts. He just missed out on getting into the Balmoral Handicap on Champions Day, so we decided to put him away and protect his mark for the Lincoln. A mile suits him perfectly and he loves tracks where he can be ridden patiently. He loves getting his toe in, too, and could have a big pot in him somewhere this year."

Dark Horse: Beccara Rose (81p): "A big filly by Sea The Stars, she ran really well twice at two when far from the finished article. She has done well over the winter and hopefully could be a smart middle-distance prospect for this year. Hopefully she'll win a novice before we look at a trial somewhere."

William Haggas

Wins-Runs in Britain in 2022	**167-671**
Highest-rated horse in training	**My Prospero** Timeform Rating 129

Star Performer: My Prospero (129): "He did little wrong last year and could well have finished unbeaten with a bit more luck. He was the second highest-rated three-year-old of 2022 with Timeform and I hope he can win a Group 1 at least."

Handicapper: Tafreej (88p): "He won nicely at Yarmouth and has a progressive profile. He was a late foal who should improve throughout the year at up to a mile."

Dark Horse: Unequal Love (unraced): "She showed plenty in the autumn last year and was very close to running when she suffered an injury which ruled her out. Seven furlongs should be a good starting point."

Richard Hannon

Wins-Runs in Britain in 2022	**110-1058**
Highest-rated horse in training	**Mojo Star** Timeform Rating 123

Star Performer: Ehraz (112): "This horse I believe could well be a Group 1 performer this year. His run in the Commonwealth Cup at Ascot where he was drawn on the outside did not show him at his best and he was still beaten only three and a half lengths by a multiple Group 1 winner. He then went on and ran again at Ascot, where he got no run, and he finished the season easily winning a conditions race at Newmarket. He has since been gelded over the winter and I am hoping for a fruitful campaign this season with him, especially on better ground."

Handicapper: Onslow Gardens (90): "He only had the three runs last season, but I am convinced that he is a really nice horse who could develop into a top-class handicapper this year. You can forget his last run as it was on soft ground, which would not have suited him. His two previous seconds were on better ground in good maidens at Newmarket (winner has since won a listed contest) and Ascot (where horses behind him have since won). That just confirms he is better than his rating of 87. He has been gelded this year."

Dark Horse: Lulworth Cove (77p): "A filly I like, she has only had the three runs. In her second run at Windsor, she was only beaten a length and three-quarters into second behind a horse who went on to win a listed contest next time. On her last run as a two-year-old she duly won her maiden at Wolverhampton. This filly will progress and win races this year."

David O'Meara

Wins-Runs in Britain in 2022	**110-904**
Highest-rated horse in training	**Escobar** Timeform Rating 120

Star Performer: Shelir (117): "He has followed up his impressive victory in the Balmoral Handicap with some high-class performances in Meydan this winter. He will be targeted at Super Saturday before returning home. Since trying hold-up tactics his form has improved and he will target multiple Group races over seven furlongs and a mile this summer."

Handicapper: Blue For You (112): "He won the Clipper Logistics Mile at York last season and was placed in the Goodwood Mile. He is a horse who showed a high level of ability in these races and may have further improvement in his second season with the yard. He will be aimed at all the major one-mile handicaps this season."

Dark Horse: Rhoscolyn (111): "He didn't get his head in front last season but is in line for a strong season in 2023. He was placed at Royal Ascot off 103 and never once dropped below a mark of 100. Starting the season on 99, he is handicapped to win some nice races based on his consistent form last year."

Kevin Ryan

Wins-Runs in Britain in 2022	**65-609**
Highest-rated horse in training	**Fonteyn** Timeform Rating 119

Star Performer: Emaraaty Ana (118): "A Group 1-winning sprinter who had another good year last season, just coming up shy of capturing another top-level success. He loves quick ground and will likely take a similar path as in previous years, tackling the top sprints."

Handicapper: Bergerac (105): "He progressed through handicaps last year, taking a big one at the Ebor Festival. He ran very well in the Ayr Gold Cup and looks set to tackle the top handicaps this season. He is a tough competitor and enjoys quicker conditions underfoot."

Dark Horse: Fast And Loose (94p): "He took a bit of time to get off the mark and looked as though he was just racing a little bit lazily early last year. Fitting headgear really helped him and he put up two fine efforts late in the season. Another year older and stronger, he could progress into a nice sprint handicapper for the year ahead."

Happy connections after Emaraaty Ana's victory in the 2021 Sprint Cup

David Simcock

Wins-Runs in Britain in 2022	**36-291**
Highest-rated horse in training	**Light Infantry** Timeform Rating 122

Star Performer: Light Infantry (122): "A talented horse who has proved himself at the top level and has arguably been unlucky. He is an extremely generous horse and finds lots off the bridle. I believe a straight course will always see him to best effect."

Handicapper: Mountain Road (99): "He improved as the year went on and it was noticeable that he started to settle better in his races as he stepped up in trip. He stays very strongly and should be seen to good effect in staying races this summer. On pedigree there is no reason why he shouldn't be better on turf."

Dark Horse: Sniper's Eye (76p): "He did lots wrong at Wolverhampton on his only start to date but has a lot of size and scope, a high cruising speed and should improve plenty when he sees big tracks over middle-distances later this year."

James Tate

Wins-Runs in Britain in 2022	**32-191**
Highest-rated horse in training	**Royal Aclaim** Timeform Rating 115

Star Performer: Royal Aclaim (115): "An exciting, lightly-raced sprinter. She is likely to start off over five furlongs in either a listed fillies' race at Bath in April or the Temple Stakes at Haydock in May. We wouldn't rule out trying six furlongs at some point."

Handicapper: Mount Athos (109p): "A big, strong four-year-old by Dark Angel who made a mockery of his opening handicap rating when scoring at Kempton in October. He is likely to reappear at the same venue at the end of March/beginning of April."

Dark Horse: Majestic Warrior (88p): "A tall, rangy, well-related Churchill colt who made light work of the opposition on his debut at Wolverhampton in January. He has now been given a break and will reappear in a novice race on turf with a penalty hopefully en route to better things."

Roger Varian

Wins-Runs in Britain in 2022	**140-639**
Highest-rated horse in training	**Eldar Eldarov** Timeform Rating 121

Star Performer: Eldar Eldarov (121): "He had an excellent three-year-old season for us with two memorable highlights. He prevailed in an incredibly tight photo-finish at Royal Ascot in the Queen's Vase and then secured classic success for the yard with victory in the St Leger. I am looking forward to him moving into Cup company and tackling staying trips."

Handicapper: Russet Gold (90): "He was progressive as a juvenile and looked very good when winning easily at Pontefract before finding conditions a bit too slow at York on his final start of the season. He has done well over the winter and hopefully he can land a nice sprint prize or two this year."

Dark Horse: Modaara (92p): "She is lightly-raced for her age after two starts and was a comfortable winner on her second outing at Chelmsford last October. She is a filly I have always liked and I am excited to see what the ceiling of her ability is."

RISING STARS

Harry Eustace

Base	**Newmarket, Suffolk**
First full licence	**2021**
First winner	**Coverham** Yarmouth 20/4/2021
Total winners	**39**
Best Flat horse trained	**Ziggy** Timeform Rating 110

2022 was a year in which Harry Eustace built on the foundations of a successful first season with a licence having taken over the running of Park Lodge Stables when his father James retired the previous year. Before that Eustace had gained plenty of experience during a four-year stint as assistant trainer to William Haggas, notably getting the opportunity to oversee the successful Australian campaign of Addeybb, but taking over from his father in Newmarket one day had always been the long-term plan. Eustace had also previously worked for other Newmarket trainers Chris Wall and Jeremy Noseda as well as gaining experience abroad in the USA and Australia. James Eustace, who trained a handful of pattern winners in a career spanning 30 years, enjoyed his best year numerically in 2003 with 19 winners, but son Harry has already bettered that total with 24 winners on the Flat in 2022 (plus one over hurdles), which was 10 more than in his first year, at a fine strike rate of 21%. Almost half of Eustace's wins came in a purple patch between mid-May and mid-June culminating in a Royal Ascot win with the trainer's very first runner at a meeting where his father had won the Hunt Cup in 1998 with Refuse To Lose. Following up under a penalty for winning at Kempton the previous week, Latin Lover beat his 26 rivals under Hayley Turner to win the Palace of Holyroodhouse Stakes. Another useful sprinter to win a good handicap for the yard was Ancient Times, in the Scottish Sprint Cup at Musselburgh, while the stable's two best handicappers, Ziggy and Makinmedoit, found their best form on the all-weather over the winter. In addition to Refuse To Lose's owner Jeff Smith, who has been a long-standing supporter of the Eustace stable, Harry Eustace has attracted important new owners such as Nick Bradley Racing, whose two-year-old filly Cite d'Or was a dual winner in 2022, and Shadwell, who will have four two-year-olds in training at Park Lodge in 2023, as well as useful four-year-old filly Alaroos formerly with Kevin Prendergast in Ireland.

James Horton

Base	**Middleham, North Yorkshire**
First full licence	**2022**
First winner	**Phantom Flight** Redcar 18/4/2022
Total winners	**18**
Best Flat horse trained	**Phantom Flight** Timeform Rating 116

As well as countless top horses, a number of professionals have also had their early careers shaped under the expertise of Sir Michael Stoute, and his former assistant James Horton followed the likes of James Fanshawe, Owen Burrows and John Ferguson when taking out a training licence of his own last season. Horton worked at Freemason Lodge for almost seven years—'a fantastic opportunity and experience for me to learn off one of the best trainers in the world'—after earlier spells working for Roger Charlton and Sir Mark Prescott, while he also named David Redvers as an important influence early on. Horton's first season with a licence was spent renting a yard from former Middleham trainer Sally Hall at Brecongill, but his permanent base will be nearby Manor House Farm, famous for being the birthplace of the last Derby winner trained in the North, the 1945 winner Dante. The property was bought by John Dance and his wife Jess late in 2020 for redevelopment as a private training centre for Horton and as a stud. Dance is part-owner of King George VI Chase winner Bravemansgame but was formerly best known for his successes with his Northern-based Flat string, headed by the tough and genuine multiple Group 1-winning filly Laurens. The new venture between the Dances and Horton got off to spectacular start, just weeks after their first runner, when they enjoyed a 140/1 treble at Redcar on Easter Monday with Phantom Flight, Asjad and Il Bandito all successful under P. J. McDonald, who partnered all bar one of the stable's 18 winners in 2022. Three-year-old Phantom Flight, winner of a novice at Redcar, had also been Horton's very first runner and ended the year as the stable's highest-rated horse, winning twice more, notably when storming to a five-length success in a handicap at York's Ebor meeting worth more than £40,000 to the winner. Il Bandito also went on to win at York, following up his Redcar success at the Dante meeting, while four-year-old Asjad finished the season rated only a pound behind Phantom Flight, he too successful at York, in the Sky Bet Sunday Series, and winning another good prize at Doncaster's St Leger meeting. Horton's other smart performers in his first season were three-year-old sprinter Sam Maximus, winner of a listed race at Newmarket, and Rhythm Master, who was runner-up in a similar event at Redcar. The stable's last four wins of the year all came from two-year-olds, with impressive Wolverhampton winner Pure Angel looking a potentially useful sprinting filly for this season.

Billy Loughnane

Attached stable	**Mark Loughnane**
First ride	**October 2022**
First winner	**Swiss Rowe** Wolverhampton 28/11/2022
Total winners in Britain	**29**
Best horse ridden	**Zealot** Timeform Rating 101

Not many of our Rising Stars have risen quite so quickly as Billy Loughnane, whose exploits over the winter were hard to keep pace with at times. The 16-year-old was virtually unknown when, little more than a month after his first ride in public, his victory on the 28/1-shot Swiss Rowe on a foggy night at Wolverhampton in November proved to be just the first of many. Swiss Rowe had been a long-standing maiden but was making only his second start for the jockey's father Mark, whose stable's excellent form over the winter meant that he was able to supply many of his son's winners. Looking excellent value for his 7 lb claim—which he soon lost in January—Loughnane quickly proved in demand from other yards and it was after the turn of the year that his career really began to take off as he became the most talked-about jockey riding on the all-weather. In January alone Loughnane clocked up 23 winners from 98 rides—only Luke Morris was busier—six clear of Danny Muscutt who was next on the list. Apart from having his claim reduced to 5 lb, Loughnane's other achievements during the month included riding his first treble, which came at Wolverhampton, repeating the feat at the same track a week later and getting another at Newcastle three days after that. Wider exposure came when he got the Ruth Carr-trained 16/1-shot Embour home by a short head on a Lingfield Saturday card televised by ITV, while Loughnane's rapid rise even resulted in him being the subject of a feature on the BBC news. Another significant winner in January was Sapphire Seas in a novice at Wolverhampton on his first ride in the Godolphin colours for Charlie Appleby. While Loughnane didn't have his first ride under Rules until last autumn, he'd already gained some valuable racing experience, along with some winners, on the pony racing circuit alongside fellow Rising Star Taylor Fisher. Loughnane says he hopes to follow in the footsteps of his 'idol' Tom Marquand, who began his riding career in the same sphere before later becoming champion apprentice. To broaden his horizons and protect his valuable claim for bigger events on turf later in the year, Loughnane took a break from the all-weather circuit to go and ride work in Florida later in the winter.

Taylor Fisher

Attached stable	**Archie Watson**
First ride	**April 2022**
First winner	**Gliding Bay** Lingfield 30/7/2022
Total winners in Britain	**27**
Best horse(s) ridden	**First Folio** Timeform Rating 111

One of last season's Rising Stars, Harry Davies, ended up losing out to Benoit de la Sayette, a former Rising Star himself, after a close battle for the title of champion apprentice in 2022. Earlier in his teens, Davies had been champion on the pony racing circuit where one of his biggest rivals was Taylor Fisher, he too a former champion in that sphere who is likewise now making a name for himself in the apprentice ranks. Fisher initially had the option of joining Davies as an apprentice with Andrew Balding but, rather than competing for the same rides at Kingsclere, opted to start out with Richard Hannon instead. But when that arrangement failed to work out, Fisher's stepfather, trainer Joe Tickle, supplied many of the then 17-year-old's early rides. However, even before he'd ridden his first winner, Fisher caught the eye of Archie Watson who signed him up in July 2022. After a number of placed efforts, Fisher got off the mark later the same month when successful aboard the Ismail Mohammed-trained Gliding Bay at an evening meeting at Lingfield. Having made that breakthrough, a stream of winners came the following month, eight of them to be precise, which included Fisher's first double, at Ffos Las, and a first winner for his Lambourn yard when Dragon Glory won a nursery at Lingfield. A victory at Chelmsford on the Gay Kelleway-trained Mukha Magic also ranks as a particularly special one among the teenager's early successes given that the other four jockeys in the race were none other than William Buick, Ryan Moore, Jamie Spencer and Andrea Atzeni. Another seven winners in September included a win on Temple Bruer in the apprentice handicap which opens Doncaster's St Leger meeting and Fisher's 7 lb allowance was put to good use on James Ferguson's smart sprinter First Folio, who'd been set to carry 10-0 in a handicap at Yarmouth. By the end of 2022, Fisher had ridden 22 winners, reducing his claim to 5 lb.

CLASSIC ANTE-POST

Timeform feature writer John Ingles takes a look at the markets for the first four classics and picks out his value bets . . .

Some classic winners are easier to find than others at an early stage in the year, and, in general, it usually pays to concentrate on the form of the top two-year-old races to identify potential winners of the 1000 and 2000 Guineas. The Derby and Oaks present more of a challenge, those races tending to be won by later-developing types who have achieved much less at two and where promise and pedigree, rather than performance, are the most important factors to weigh up. A good bit of luck doesn't go amiss, either, of course! Anyway, last year's recommendations included Coroebus, 5/1 winner of the 2000 Guineas, and Desert Crown, advised here at 40/1 each way, who won the Derby as the 5/2 favourite. So, let's hope there's another classic winner or two in this year's preview.

2000 Guineas

You could hardly get two 2000 Guineas contenders with more differing profiles than the Ballydoyle pair disputing ante-post favouritism, **Little Big Bear** and **Auguste Rodin**. On the one hand, Little Big Bear was all speed and precocity at two, the Windsor Castle Stakes winner's campaign ending spectacularly, but also prematurely in early-August, with a seven-length beating of solid yardstick Persian Force in the Phoenix Stakes. A physically imposing sort with stamina on his dam's side, Little Big Bear nonetheless faces a very different test in the Guineas, even if reported to be fully recovered from the foot injury which put paid to an autumn campaign. Aidan O'Brien has completed the Futurity-Guineas double with another son of Deep Impact, Saxon Warrior, but the big question for Auguste Rodin, in contrast, is will the Guineas be a sufficient test for a colt who looked more like a Derby horse when forging clear to win the Futurity Trophy on heavy ground, following two wins on soft in Ireland.

Neither the National Stakes nor the Dewhurst Stakes was as good some of the recent renewals of those contests, though the winners of both races, **Al Riffa** and **Chaldean** respectively, are smart colts. Chaldean completed a four-timer at Newmarket after wins in the Acomb Stakes and Champagne Stakes and is an uncomplicated sort who showed a willing attitude to make all in the Dewhurst and hold off the Richmond Stakes winner **Royal Scotsman** by a head. Despite that close margin, the latter is twice

Nostrum looks a big contender for the 2000 Guineas

the price of Chaldean but in an open year it could be worth giving the Sir Michael Stoute-trained Dewhurst third **Nostrum** another chance.

The market couldn't split the Juddmonte colts Nostrum and Chaldean before the Dewhurst, with Nostrum looking an exciting prospect after winning a maiden at Sandown (won by future 2000 Guineas winner Kameko a few years back) and the Tattersalls Stakes despite still looking very green. The Dewhurst, in which he took a keen hold, might have been a bit too much for him, therefore, so soon in his career but Nostrum is a really good-looking son of Kingman who could shake up the Guineas market in a trial such as the Craven Stakes if more the finished article on his return.

Noble Style and **Sakheer** are others prominent in the 2000 Guineas betting after looking good prospects at two but, like Little Big Bear, neither are yet proven beyond six furlongs. Noble Style, another son of Kingman but from a speedy family, was unbeaten in three starts for Charlie Appleby but a bout of colic meant he wasn't seen out after winning the Gimcrack Stakes in which a below-form Royal Scotsman, in fifth, finished behind him for a second time. Less of Sakheer was seen than planned too as he was withdrawn from the Dewhurst with a dirty scope after being supplemented. Both his wins were gained impressively, notably when outclassing his rivals in a steadily-run Mill Reef Stakes.

Recommendation: Nostrum (12/1)

1000 Guineas

The ante-post betting for the 1000 Guineas would suggest it has the makings of a two-horse race, especially in the absence of Commissioning, who has been retired due to injury since she capped an unbeaten two-year-old campaign with victory in the Fillies' Mile. The other two horses in question are **Tahiyra** and **Meditate**, both of whom hold strong claims. Twice-raced favourite Tahiyra almost certainly has the most potential of the trio having won both her starts for Dermot Weld most impressively. The way she beat the previously unbeaten Meditate without coming under the whip in the Moyglare Stud Stakes makes the half-sister to her stable's high-class filly Tarnawa a really exciting prospect stepping up to a mile.

Dermot Weld has had only one runner in either of the Newmarket classics this century but made it count when Refuse To Bend won the 2000 Guineas in 2003. It would be typical of Weld's selective approach if he struck in another Guineas 20 years later, but there's no getting away from Aidan O'Brien's record when it comes to the Newmarket classics, which includes winning five of the last seven editions of the 1000 Guineas.

That sways the vote in favour of Meditate, who thrived on her racing last year, her quite busy juvenile campaign typical of some of O'Brien's former 1000 Guineas

Meditate is well on top in the Breeders' Cup Juvenile Fillies Turf

winners. She was better than ever when stepping up to a mile for the first time in the Breeders' Cup Juvenile Fillies Turf, settling matters with a fine turn of foot, with the less battle-hardened Oh So Sharp Stakes winner **Midnight Mile** staying on for fourth. Meditate would have to turn the Moyglare form around if meeting Tahiyra again, but firmer ground at Newmarket (it was heavy at the Curragh) could help her do just that. Speedy enough to win the Albany Stakes at Royal Ascot earlier on, Meditate showed she needed further by the autumn when beaten by **Lezoo**, who looks a sprinter rather than a Guineas filly, in the Cheveley Park Stakes prior to the Breeders' Cup.

Meditate's stablemate **Statuette** wasn't seen out after June but shouldn't be overlooked as she made a fine impression, winning both her starts, including the Group 2 Airlie Stud Stakes at the Curragh. By US triple crown winner Justify, she's bred to see out the mile better than close relative Tenebrism, the beaten favourite in last year's 1000 Guineas.

Recommendation: Meditate (4/1)

The Derby

As noted above, **Auguste Rodin** shot to the head of the Derby betting after his clear-cut success in testing conditions in the Futurity Trophy and, with every chance of staying a mile and a half on pedigree—his dam Rhododendron was second in Enable's Oaks—it's hard to argue he shouldn't be favourite on the evidence available so far. But as he's generally on offer at 11/4 at the time of writing in what amounts to a largely one-horse book, there's plenty of choice when it comes to some longer-priced alternatives. Auguste Rodin's odds could contract further with a promising run at Newmarket, much like those of his stable's 2021 Futurity Trophy winner Luxembourg did after finishing third in the 2000 Guineas, though he never made it to Epsom.

Some of Aidan O'Brien's other Derby possibles ran good races in France in the autumn, with **Continuous** making it two from two in the Group 3 Prix Thomas Bryon, **Denmark** finishing a close second in a sales race at the Arc meeting and **Espionage** going down by a head to Donnacha O'Brien's National Stakes runner-up **Proud And Regal** in the Criterium International. By Galileo out of a Ribblesdale winner, Espionage makes plenty of appeal on pedigree, but the pick from Ballydoyle is the colt who beat Espionage into second when the pair made their debuts at Galway in September. **Alexandroupolis** ran out a ready winner once getting a clear run in a race won by his stable's top stayer Kyprios in 2020 and is sure to progress over middle-distances, being by Camelot out of a half-sister to one of Ballydoyle's St Leger winners Kew Gardens. He's one to look out for in a Derby trial.

Charlie Appleby has put up the most resistance to O'Brien in the Derby in recent seasons, winning it with Masar and Adayar, and he looks to have a number of colts who could make up into Epsom types. The likes of Zetland Stakes winner **Flying Honours** and Breeders' Cup Juvenile Turf runner-up **Silver Knott**, earlier successful in the Solario Stakes and Autumn Stakes, have already shown their hand at Group level, but Godolphin have others in the 'could be anything' category. They include Adayar's brother **Military Order** who won a novice at Newmarket on his second start and another Frankel colt, **Measured Time**, a half-brother to last year's Breeders' Cup Turf winner Rebel's Romance, who was a four-length winner of a maiden at Kempton on his debut in February. The one who appeals most, though, is **Imperial Emperor** who might not have won the strongest of Newmarket maidens on his debut in October but there was a lot to like about the way he went about it, giving the impression that he has scope for plenty of improvement. His pedigree suggests as much, too, as he's out of a Grade 1-winning half-sister to Godolphin's top-class middle-distance horse Ghaiyyath and by the same sire, Dubawi.

Recommendations: Alexandroupolis (25/1), Imperial Emperor (16/1)

Imperial Emperor impressed when making a winning debut at Newmarket

The Oaks

Tahiyra, who heads the ante-post betting for this race as well as the 1000 Guineas, should have no trouble staying the Oaks trip if taking after her half-sister Tarnawa, who finished down the field as a 20/1 shot in the 2019 Oaks but later proved herself at the top level over a mile and a half with wins in the Prix Vermeille and Breeders' Cup Turf.

Last year's Oaks was fought out by Tuesday and Emily Upjohn from the stables of Aidan O'Brien and John and Thady Gosden who, between them, have now won the last nine editions of the race. There's no standout contender from Ballydoyle at this stage, though Tuesday's sister **Delightful** makes obvious appeal on pedigree. However, having won a nursery at Leopardstown from a Turf Club mark of 86 on her final start last year, she clearly has a lot of improving to do to merit consideration. On the other hand, it's not hard to imagine **Victorium**'s odds (25/1 at the time of writing) being slashed were she to make a winning debut in the spring. She's by Deep Impact and the first foal out of the 2016 Oaks winner Minding, sister to Tuesday and Delightful.

The Gosdens, on the other hand, even in the absence of Commissioning, have a trio of likely fillies who won their sole starts at two, something they have in common with a couple of the stable's Oaks winners, Taghrooda and Enable, as well as Emily Upjohn. The Godolphin-owned **Bridestones** looked a good prospect when showing a sharp turn of foot in soft ground to win a novice at Yarmouth in October with plenty in hand. She's out of the Fillies' Mile winner White Moonstone and by Teofilo so bred to improve over further. **Soul Sister**, a daughter of Frankel and the smart French winner up to a mile and a quarter Dream Peace, won in even more testing conditions at Doncaster the same month, and while she only got home by a head, she overcame greenness to get the better of a more experienced rival as the pair finished clear. **Inner Space** made her winning debut at Kempton in November, impressing with the way she quickened clear after making all. She too makes plenty of appeal on pedigree, by Siyouni out of her stable's very smart Fillies' And Mares' Stakes winner Journey.

Fillies with similar profiles from other yards to mention include **Bluestocking**, her trainer Ralph Beckett himself the trainer of two Oaks winners already. The daughter of Camelot was green for her Salisbury debut but won going away. Joseph O'Brien's **Sandy Creek** is a Frankel close relative to last year's Derby contender Stone Age and shaped very well when second to Ballydoyle's future Marcel Boussac third **Never Ending Story** in a maiden at the Curragh in June on her only outing. The bare form of **Rainbow Sky**'s winning debut at Kempton for Charlie Appleby in November is nothing out of the ordinary, but the daughter of Sea The Stars who cost 1.5m guineas as a yearling looks capable of making significant progress.

Recommendations: Inner Space, Soul Sister (both 33/1)

TOP ON TIME

Timing expert Graeme North highlights seven horses who have fared well on the clock and are of interest for the coming season.

Artistic Star (Ire)   91p

3 b.c. Galileo (Ire) – Nechita (Aus) (Fastnet Rock (Aus))

Artistic Star showed more than enough when making a successful debut at Nottingham in October to think he might provide the late Galileo, the outstanding stallion of the recent past, with another Group winner. Sent off an unconsidered 16/1 shot in a maiden featuring several promising sorts and which had been won the previous year by the St Leger winner Eldar Eldarov, Artistic Star was never far away and ran on strongly after being produced to lead entering the final furlong. A 91 timefigure is extremely high for a newcomer over a mile at the end of the season and, being a brother to winners over a mile and a half, he's sure to leave his very promising debut effort behind when tackling the Derby distance. *Ralph Beckett*

The form of Enfjaar's Newmarket maiden win has worked out well

Enfjaar (Ire) 94p
3 b.c. Lope de Vega (Ire) – Tesoro (Ire) (Galileo (Ire))

Few two-year-old maidens worked out as well last season as the one won by Enfjaar at Newmarket in October. Neither he nor the runner-up Arabian Storm have been seen since at the time of writing, but the next three home all won next time which augurs well for the selection given how well on top he was at the line. Indeed, the sectionals provided by Course Track show that he ran the last furlong much faster than his rivals and, though he isn't short of speed, the Galileo influence on the distaff side of his pedigree suggests he'll make a stack of improvement when stepping up to a mile. Enfjaar looks the part, being a tall colt, and he was very settled in the preliminaries despite being fitted with a hood for his debut. Kinross won the same race back in 2019 and it's not fanciful to think that Enfjaar has a future in pattern company, too. *Roger Varian*

Hosanna Power (Ire) 83p
3 ch.c. Frankel – Belle Josephine (Dubawi (Ire))

Hosanna Power made a promising debut in a late-season maiden at Doncaster that already looks strong form, and he looks set to make up into a good handicapper at least in 2023, very much the type who will thrive over a mile and a half and beyond. Unfancied at 16/1 on Town Moor, Hosanna Power was soon close up but seemed to take some time to grasp what was required of him when asked and didn't really make any inroads until late on when the penny really dropped. An opening timefigure of 83 is a solid base to build from and, being by Frankel out of a Dubawi mare who has thrown a couple of useful performers, including the smart stayer Mildenberger, Hosanna Power ought to progress well for a trainer who excels with such types. *Sir Michael Stoute*

Maljoom (Ire) 121p
4 b.c. Caravaggio (USA) – Nictate (Ire) (Teofilo (Ire))

Maljoom might still be awaiting his first domestic Group success, but there are good reasons for thinking he was the best three-year-old miler in training last season. Maljoom already has a Group 2 win to his name—in the German equivalent of the 2000 Guineas which he won comprehensively despite a slow start and a poor position in a slowly-run race—but it was on his final outing in the St James's Palace Stakes at Royal Ascot that he gave an inkling as to how good he might be. Hemmed in on the rail with seemingly nowhere to go, Maljoom made up all of five lengths inside the final furlong, emerging with an 8 lb better upgrade than any of his rivals from that point and looking a most unlucky loser. He missed a target later in the season after a dirty scope but looked top class at Ascot and ought to be not long in making up for lost time. *William Haggas*

Maljoom seems sure to win more good races in 2023

Sandy Creek (Ire)   90p

3 b.f. Frankel – Bonanza Creek (Ire) (Anabaa (USA))

One of the most promising debuts from a two-year-old filly last season, on either side of the Irish Sea, came from Sandy Creek in a maiden at the Curragh in June which has traditionally been a strong and informative contest. Won in 2021 by the subsequent Moyglare Stud Stakes winner Discoveries, with the Oaks and Breeders' Cup Filly and Mare Turf winner Tuesday back in second, the latest edition went to Never Ending Story, who went on to win the Group 3 Silver Flash Stakes before finishing third in the Prix Marcel Boussac. However, it was the performance of the runner-up Sandy Creek that really took the eye. Held up off the pace, she still had plenty to do with two furlongs to run but finished with a flourish without being knocked about. Sectional upgrades on top of a good 84 timefigure suggest Sandy Creek was the 'moral winner' of that contest and, being a close relation of the smart mile-and-a-quarter winner Stone Age, she is sure to improve markedly given the chance to tackle that distance herself. She holds an entry in the Irish Oaks. *Joseph O'Brien, Ireland*

Tarjeeh (Ire) 103p
3 b.c. Churchill (Ire) – Myturn (Ire) (Rock of Gibraltar (Ire))

Owen Burrows had something of a standout year domestically in 2022 from a reduced string, sending out 21 winners from just 67 runners at a remarkable 31% strike rate, and he has a potentially very smart colt in Tarjeeh for 2023. Considering his sire Churchill has a very modest record with his first-time-out runners, Tarjeeh's debut fourth over an inadequate six furlongs at Windsor from the widest draw of all in a race which worked out very well was a very encouraging effort, and he left that well behind at Newbury next time when upped a furlong in trip. As at Windsor, where Total Performance data had him running easily the quickest final furlong of all the runners, he came home fastest of all at Newbury according to Course Track while posting a useful 95 timefigure into the bargain. The five who followed Tarjeeh home all finished either first or second next time and, with plenty of stamina in his pedigree, he looks capable of making considerable progress when stepped up to a mile and a quarter or so. *Owen Burrows*

Troon (Ire) 91p
3 b.c. Gleneagles (Ire) – Sacred Harp (Oasis Dream)

Eve Johnson Houghton edged up her seasonal tally of winners marginally to 47 in 2022 and must be in with a good chance of topping 50 for the first time in 2023. There tends to be more quality in her string among the three-year-olds and older horses, but there have been signs in recent seasons that there is a greater focus on juvenile talent, and, in Troon, she uncovered a potentially smart prospect at Kempton in October. That race didn't look the strongest contest, admittedly, but Troon was able to not only overcome the widest stall in a 14-runner field on his debut, but he also ran an eye-catching final sectional as he stormed home from last to first. It's interesting to note that the other newcomer Mindthegap, who was drawn two stalls inside him and was also out the back on the home turn, showed vastly improved form when winning next time, and the likelihood is that Troon, who emerged with a 10 lb better upgrade, will do the same. Trips around a mile seem likely to suit him best. *Eve Johnson Houghton*

FIRST-SEASON SIRES

John Ingles runs the rule over some of the sires whose first runners are set to hit the track this season.

Advertise (Highest Timeform rating 125)

Showcasing – Furbelow (Pivotal)

There were obvious excuses for the only two occasions that Advertise didn't give his running—the trip in the 2000 Guineas and the soft ground in the British Champions Sprint Stakes. Otherwise, Advertise was a model of consistency, finishing first or second in all his other starts. At two his big wins came in the July Stakes and Phoenix Stakes, while he ran well in defeat behind Calyx in the Coventry Stakes at Royal Ascot and when finding only champion two-year-old Too Darn Hot too strong in the Dewhurst Stakes. That good effort over seven furlongs prompted his 2000 Guineas bid the following spring, but it was when blinkered and back at sprint trips that Advertise ran his best races at three, winning the Commonwealth Cup and Prix Maurice de Gheest and coming second to Ten Sovereigns in the July Cup in between. Advertise began his stud career at the National Stud for £25,000, but this year he returned to Martyn Meade's Manton Park as part of his former trainer's new stallion operation. By the Gimcrack Stakes winner Showcasing, Advertise has a reported 103 two-year-olds so seems sure to make an impact even if that's the smallest crop of the six stallions profiled here. His stand-out yearling in terms of price was a colt out of the Nell Gwyn Stakes runner-up Squash who fetched 500,000 guineas at Tattersalls, while he also had a filly out of a half-sister to the smart French miler Stunning Spirit sell for €300,000 at Goffs.

Blue Point (Ire) (131)

Shamardal (USA) – Scarlett Rose (Royal Applause)

Godolphin's top-class sprinter Blue Point will probably be best remembered for his unbeaten campaign as a five-year-old. After completing a hat-trick in Dubai early in the year in the Group 1 Al Quoz Sprint, he went on to complete a rare double at Royal Ascot, wearing down Battaash for the second year running over the stiff five furlongs in the King's Stand Stakes and then following up in the Diamond Jubilee Stakes four days later. While it was disappointing that Blue Point was then retired mid-season at the height of his powers, he had achieved plenty already, winning Group races in all four seasons that he raced. He was smart at two, winning the Gimcrack Stakes impressively by three lengths—in between second places in the Richmond Stakes and Middle Park Stakes—and finishing a respectable third to Churchill in the Dewhurst Stakes on his only try at seven furlongs. As well as his later Royal Ascot victories, as a three-year-old

Blue Point won four Group 1 sprints in his illustrious career

he was third to Caravaggio and Harry Angel in a deep edition of the Commonwealth Cup and gained Group 3 wins at the same course in the Pavilion Stakes and Bengough Stakes. A notably speedy son of Shamardal, he joined his late sire at Kildangan Stud at a fee of €45,000, resulting in a huge first crop of 161 two-year-olds, six of those with Blue Point's own trainer Charlie Appleby. Among his yearlings who went through the ring, M. V. Magnier paid €420,000 for a filly out of a half-sister to King's Stand Stakes winner Profitable.

Inns of Court (Ire) (124)

Invincible Spirit (Ire) – Learned Friend (Ger) (Seeking The Gold (USA))

A Group 1 win eluded Inns of Court in a career that saw him win his only start at two, over seven furlongs on Chantilly's polytrack, and race on for Andre Fabre and Godolphin until the age of five. But he went very close on two occasions, beaten a short head by stablemate Al Wukair in the Prix Jacques le Marois at three and going down by the same margin to the filly One Master in the Prix de la Foret a year later. While Inns of Court had good form at a mile, all his wins came at shorter trips, including a couple of

Group 3 victories over seven furlongs at three and another, in the Prix de Ris-Orangis at Maisons-Laffitte, over six furlongs at four. Inns of Court ended up sprinting full-time, with the last of his seven wins coming in the Group 2 Prix du Gros-Chene at Chantilly over five furlongs, as good as any performance he put up in his career. With the exception of one run in Hong Kong, Inns of Court raced entirely in France but being a son of Invincible Spirit no doubt accounts for the considerable support he's had from Irish breeders. Inns of Court has a reported 168 two-year-olds conceived at a fee of €7,500 which gives him every chance of emulating fellow Tally-Ho Stud stallions Cotai Glory and Mehmas, both of whom have been leading first-season sires in recent years. He had a half-sister to Phoenix Stakes winner Ebro River sell for 175,000 guineas at Tattersalls, while Amo Racing went to €170,000 at Goffs for a half-brother to their useful two-year-old sprinter of last year Persian Force.

Soldier's Call (119)
Showcasing – Dijarvo (Iceman)

Unlike the other son of Showcasing profiled here, Advertise, there was never any temptation to try Soldier's Call over longer trips. He was an out-and-out five-furlong performer whose four career wins for Archie Watson all came at two. After beating a huge field in the Windsor Castle Stakes at Royal Ascot, he also made all in the Prix d'Arenberg and Flying Childers Stakes, though gained as much credit for taking third against older rivals in a very tight finish to the Prix de l'Abbaye won by Mabs Cross. While Soldier's Call failed to add to those wins at three, he showed he'd trained on by being placed in two more top sprints, finishing third to Blue Point and Battaash in the King's Stand Stakes and runner-up to the latter when he broke the course record in the Nunthorpe Stakes. Soldier's Call stood his first season at Ballyhane Stud at a fee of €10,000 and is another who will have plenty of ammunition with 121 two-year-olds in his first crop which should ensure that he's one of the quickest first-season sires to get winners on the board. His highest-priced yearlings included a colt from the speedy family of King's Stand Stakes winner Dominica bought for £105,000 at Doncaster and a half-sister to useful sprinter Last Crusader, a listed winner at York last season, who sold for €120,000 at Goffs.

Ten Sovereigns (Ire) (126)
No Nay Never (USA) – Seeking Solace (Exceed And Excel (Aus))

No Nay Never had a tremendous season with his two-year-olds last year, a group which included the likes of Little Big Bear, Blackbeard and Meditate, but he was also the leading first-season sire of 2018 thanks in no small part to the exploits of his smart two-year-old Ten Sovereigns who, like Blackbeard, ended his juvenile campaign with

Ten Sovereigns enjoyed his career highlight when winning the July Cup

victory in the Middle Park Stakes. Ten Sovereigns was unbeaten in three starts at two having only made his debut about a month before the Middle Park, but he was stretched by the longer trip when sent off favourite for the 2000 Guineas, finishing fifth to stablemate Magna Grecia. Reverting to six furlongs for the rest of the year, Ten Sovereigns ran a career best when putting up a high-class performance to win the July Cup, staying on strongly to give a two-and-three-quarter-length beating to Advertise. Starting his stud career at Coolmore at a fee of €25,000, Ten Sovereigns continues the theme of very large crops with 149 two-year-olds to run for him. His top-priced yearling, sold at Goffs for €500,000, is a speedily-bred colt out of a half-sister to the Flying Childers Stakes winner Sand Vixen, while a filly who fetched €300,000 is another sharp type on pedigree as she's closely related to Ballydoyle's smart sprinter Cadamosto (by No Nay Never). Ten Sovereigns covered a number of more stoutly-bred mares, too, plenty of them by Galileo.

Too Darn Hot (127)

Dubawi (Ire) – Dar Re Mi (Singspiel (Ire))

Too Darn Hot has less of a speedy profile than the above-named first-season sires, but that didn't stop him becoming the champion two-year-old in an unbeaten campaign in 2018 which included wins in the Solario Stakes and Champagne Stakes before giving a two-and-three-quarter-length beating to Advertise in the Dewhurst Stakes. A strong favourite over the winter for the 2000 Guineas, Too Darn Hot had to miss that race after a setback in the spring and reappeared instead with a second place in the Dante Stakes. But rather than taking the Derby route from there, Too Darn Hot was dropped back in trip for the rest of his campaign, and while a beaten favourite again in the Irish 2000 Guineas and St James's Palace Stakes, he restored his reputation with a couple more Group 1 wins in the Prix Jean Prat at Deauville and in the Sussex Stakes where he turned the tables on his Royal Ascot conqueror Circus Maximus. The Breeders' Cup Mile was his intended end-of-year target, but a hairline fracture brought his racing career to an end. Retired to Dalham Hall Stud at a fee of £50,000, Too Darn Hot has 120 two-year-olds in his first crop, and while he might not be the fastest into his stride, he's sure to get his fair share of winners in the second half of the season. His highest-priced yearling was a colt out of the May Hill Stakes winner Turret Rocks bought by David Redvers for 600,000 guineas at Tattersalls, while a filly out of a half-sister to Group 1 winners Japan and Mogul was a 320,000 guineas purchase by Shadwell.

Best of the rest

Two more sires who look all set to get plenty of winners with their first crop of two-year-olds are **Land Force** (109) and **Calyx** (124), both of whom were precocious types themselves and have three-figure books to help get them off to a good start. Land Force, a son of No Nay Never, won three races at two for Aidan O'Brien, notably the Richmond Stakes, and had just the one run at three in Australia. His first crop at Highclere Stud were conceived at a fee of £6,500. Injuries at both two and three restricted Calyx to just two appearances in each of those seasons and he never got an opportunity to prove himself the top-notch sprinter he looked like being as a result, though he beat Advertise in the Coventry Stakes just a week after making his debut and was an impressive winner of the Group 3 Pavilion Stakes back at Ascot on his return at three before an odds-on defeat in the Sandy Lane Stakes brought an abrupt end to his career. Coolmore snapped up the son of Kingman for stallion duties and his first-season fee was €22,500, though he's standing for less than half that this year.

Invincible Spirit is very well represented in this year's batch of first-season sires, and besides Inns of Court, **Invincible Army** (120) and **Eqtidaar** (117) are two more sprinting sons of his with their first two-year-olds in 2023. The pair actually met in competition more than once, Invincible Army coming out on top in the Sirenia Stakes at Kempton at two, and while he failed to make the breakthrough at Group 1 level, he notched a Group 2 success at four in the Duke of York Stakes and also landed another Group race on the all-weather, the Chipchase Stakes at Newcastle. The more lightly-raced Eqtidaar was runner-up to Invincible Army in the Pavilion Stakes at Ascot but had that rival down the field when putting up a career-best effort to win the Commonwealth Cup.

Invincible Spirit is also the sire of **Magna Grecia** (124), another well-represented Coolmore stallion with 109 two-year-olds from a first crop conceived at a fee of €22,500. A half-brother to St Mark's Basilica, Magna Grecia raced only six times but won the Futurity Trophy on his final two-year-old start before winning the 2000 Guineas in Too Darn Hot's absence as Ballydoyle's second string to Ten Sovereigns. Magna Grecia's half-brother to 2000 Guineas winner Poetic Flare sold for 300,000 guineas at Tattersalls in October. The Irish National Stud's **Phoenix of Spain** (122), by Lope de Vega, was beaten a head by Magna Grecia in the Futurity Trophy having won the Acomb Stakes earlier at two, and he too went on to classic success at three when making just about all for a surprise win in the Irish 2000 Guineas from Too Darn Hot with Magna Grecia only fifth.

Other sires of note with their first runners in 2023 include middle-distance performers **Masar** (125), **Waldgeist** (132) and **Study of Man** (122), all of whom will most likely need the longer two-year-old races to start before they start to make more of an impact. Derby winner Masar has a large crop of 104 two-year-olds, however, and was quick enough to make a winning debut over six furlongs in May, later winning the Solario Stakes at two and the Craven Stakes early at three. Waldgeist was a five-year-old when signing off with a career-best effort to beat Enable in the Prix de l'Arc de Triomphe, but the son of Galileo had also been a Group 1 winner at two in the Criterium de Saint-Cloud. Lanwades Stud's Prix du Jockey Club winner Study of Man has a small crop compared to most of his contemporaries but, by Deep Impact from the family of top sire Kingmambo, he's as well-bred as any of this year's first-season sires.

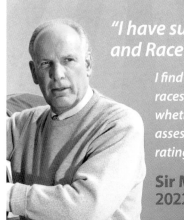

SECTION

TIMEFORM'S VIEW

Chosen from the Timeform Formbook, here is Timeform's detailed analysis—compiled by our team of race reporters and supplemented by observations from Timeform's handicappers—of a selection of key juvenile races from last year.

DEAUVILLE Sunday August 21
GOOD

Darley Prix Morny - Finale des Darley Series (Group 1) (Colts And Fillies)

Pos	Draw	Btn	Horse	Age	Wgt	Eq	Trainer	Jockey	SP
1	1		BLACKBEARD (IRE)	2	9-0		Aidan O'Brien, Ireland	Ryan Moore	13/10
2	5	½	PERSIAN FORCE (IRE)	2	9-0		Richard Hannon	Frankie Dettori	12/10f
3	3	1½	THE ANTARCTIC (IRE)	2	9-0		Aidan O'Brien, Ireland	Ioritz Mendizabal	81/10
4	4	2	MANHATTAN JUNGLE (IRE)	2	8-11		Amy Murphy	Tony Piccone	15/1
5	2	2½	THE RIDLER	2	9-0		Richard Fahey	Christophe Soumillon	66/10

5 ran Race Time 1m 09.91 Winning Owner: D.Smith,Mrs J.Magnier,M.Tabor,Westerberg

A Prix Morny notable for the absence of any French runners but a straightforward one to assess with all bar The Ridler running pretty much to form, while Persian Force's prominent showing underlined how good Little Big Bear's performance was in leaving him for dead at the Curragh earlier in the month; Blackbeard and The Ridler raced up the stand rail with the rest a bit wider on the track, the winner a first for Ballydoyle since Aidan O'Brien won this 3 times in 4 years around the millennium, notably with Blackbeard's great grandsire Johannesburg. **Blackbeard** only needed to repeat his Robert Papin form to follow up, taking his record to 5 wins from 7 starts; led on the stand rail from the 1 stall, quickened with the runner-up over 1f out and was always holding that one off in the final 1f, driven out; not for the first time he acted up behind the stalls and got warm but did nothing wrong in the race, his future prospects dependent largely on plans for the likes of stablemate Little Big Bear, who left Persian Force for dead last time, and Gimcrack winner Noble Style who'd be a tough opponent in the Middle Park. **Persian Force** ran up to his best but found a Ballydoyle colt too strong again, though made more of a race of it than he was able to do against Little Big Bear last time; tracked pace, typically travelled well, quickened with the winner over 1f out, kept on but always being held. **The Antarctic** had been no match for Blackbeard in the Robert Papin 2 starts ago and ran creditably to be placed behind his stablemate again; waited with last of the trio who raced away from the rail, outpaced under 2f out, ran on final 1f. **Manhattan Jungle** had a bit to find against these colts but wasn't disgraced; led the trio who raced away from the rail but gradually left behind by the principals from 2f out. **The Ridler**, was bidding to follow in the footsteps of stablemate Perfect Power who completed the Norfolk-Morny double last year, but his form last time isn't working out and he did nothing for it himself upped in trip after 10 weeks off; tracked Blackbeard on the stand rail, effort 2f out, beaten final 1f.

CURRAGH Sunday September 11
HEAVY

Moyglare Stud Stakes (Group 1)

Pos	Draw	Btn	Horse	Age	Wgt	Eq	Trainer	Jockey	SP
1	7		TAHIYRA (IRE)	2	9-2		D. K. Weld, Ireland	C. D. Hayes	10/3
2	12	2¼	MEDITATE (IRE)	2	9-2		Aidan O'Brien, Ireland	Ryan Moore	1/1f
3	3	4½	ETERNAL SILENCE (USA)	2	9-2		Mrs J. Harrington, Ireland	Shane Foley	50/1
4	6	2	NEVER ENDING STORY (IRE)	2	9-2		Aidan O'Brien, Ireland	W. M. Lordan	9/1
5	5	½	LA DOLCE VITA (IRE)	2	9-2		D. A. O'Brien, Ireland	G. M. Ryan	100/1
6	9	1¼	PAPILIO (IRE)	2	9-2		J. A. Stack, Ireland	Jamie Spencer	14/1
7	11	1¼	GAN TEORAINN (IRE)	2	9-2	(b)	J. S. Bolger, Ireland	K. J. Manning	125/1
8	8	nk	THORNBROOK (IRE)	2	9-2		J. P. O'Brien, Ireland	Declan McDonogh	17/2
9	1	nk	AMAZING SHOW (IRE)	2	9-2		G. M. Lyons, Ireland	C. T. Keane	40/1
10	2	sh	SHELTON (IRE)	2	9-2		P. Twomey, Ireland	William James Lee	20/1
11	4	2	LAKOTA SIOUX (IRE)	2	9-2		Charlie & Mark Johnston	Richard Kingscote	14/1

11 ran Race Time 1m 29.16 Closing Sectional (3.00f): 37.4s (102.2%) Winning Owner: H. H. Aga Khan

Most had plenty to find but the favourite Meditate lined up as the season's leading 2-y-o filly and surely ran at least as well as previously, finishing well clear of the rest but no match for the once-raced Tahiyra, who put up one of the best ever performances in a race with some notable names on its roll of honour, the form substantiated by a strung-out finish and a faster time than the colts managed in the National Stakes 35 minutes later. **Tahiyra** overcame the steep rise in class 7 weeks on from her winning debut, looking by far the best juvenile filly seen out this season and one of the best 2-y-os around full stop; settled mid-field, smooth headway under 2f out, quickened to lead last ½f without rider going for whip, impressive and value extra; she reportedly won't run again this season and looks a rightful favourite for next year's Guineas, while the stamina in her pedigree—her half-sister Tarnawa was high class over middle distances—makes her a most exciting prospect indeed. **Meditate** might have lost her unbeaten record but ran her best race yet on form, beating the rest hollow and going down only to a top-class prospect; disputed lead, quickened 2f out, headed last ½f, clear of remainder; in Tahiyra's likely absence, she looks well up to winning a Group 1 this autumn, including over 1m. **Eternal Silence** ran well up futher in grade, the way she stuck at it back down in trip suggesting she'll do better again back around 1m, certainly looking to take after the stamina-laden dam's side of her breeding; held up, headway over 1f out, ran on. **Never Ending Story** was chief among those better than the result, never getting enough room to show what she could do; mid-field, travelled well, not clear run over 1f out, bumped entering final 1f, no chance after, finished with running left; she may well improve further and could win another pattern race this backend. **La Dolce Vita** ran respectably considering she's rather exposed, a more patient ride helping her see things out better, not that she was ever a threat; held up, effort out wide 2f out, kept on. **Papilio** wasn't seen to best effect up further in grade; steadied at the start, held up, effort on inner under 2f out, met some trouble, never a threat. **Gan Teorainn** in first-time blinkers, faced a stiff task in this grade; prominent, ridden soon after 3f out, bumped approaching final 1f, weakened. **Thornbrook** was below form on softer ground than before, having finished just a length behind Meditate here the time before; close up, effort 2f out, weakened final 1f. **Amazing Show** faced a stiffffer task;

mid-division, met some trouble approaching final 1f, never a threat. **Shelton** on softer ground than previously, underperformed; prominent, effort 2f out, faded. **Lakota Sioux** underperformed, possibly unsuited by conditions; disputed lead, weakened final 1f.

Goffs Vincent O'Brien National Stakes (Group 1)

Pos	Draw	Btn	Horse	Age	Wgt	Eq	Trainer	Jockey	SP
1	5		AL RIFFA (FR)	2	9-5		J. P. O'Brien, Ireland	D. B. McMonagle	9/1
2	6	1¼	PROUD AND REGAL (IRE)	2	9-5		D. A. O'Brien, Ireland	G. M. Ryan	9/1
3	2	½	SHARTASH (IRE)	2	9-5		John Patrick Murtagh, Ireland	Ben Martin Coen	14/1
4	3	1¼	AESOP'S FABLES (IRE)	2	9-5		Aidan O'Brien, Ireland	Ryan Moore	8/13f
5	1	1¼	HANS ANDERSEN	2	9-5		Aidan O'Brien, Ireland	Seamie Heffernan	9/1
6	4	2½	MARBAAN	2	9-5		Charlie Fellowes	Jamie Spencer	7/1

6 ran   Race Time 1m 29.31   Closing Sectional (3.00f): 36.85s (103.9%)   Winning Owner: Mr Jassim Bin Ali Al Attiyah

All 6 lined up with varying degrees of potential and it was the only one yet to contest a pattern race that found the most improvement, Al Riffa looking very good value for his last-to-first success, though a fairly bunched finish means the form is just smart, a bit below the overall standard for a race that's seen 1 or 2 exceptional performances in recent years. **Al Riffa** was much improved to overcome the steep rise in grade 6 weeks on from his C&D maiden win, doing well to come from last to first; held up, headway under pressure out wide over 1f out, stayed on to lead final 100 yds, driven out; he's sure to be suited by 1m this year and further still next, which makes him a very exciting prospect. **Proud And Regal** ran a fine race as he reversed form with the 2 Ballydoyle colts that had finished ahead of him in the Futurity here, under strong pressure before his rivals but responding well, underlining that he's going to be suited by 1m and beyond; in touch, ridden over 2f out, stayed on, took second final 100 yds. **Shartash** ran his best race, no surprise the longer trip suited considering his pedigree and the way he'd been shaping; mid-division, shaken up 2f out, challenged final 1f, one paced. **Aesop's Fables** went off odds-on but lost his unbeaten record, having no obvious excuses the way things went, though perhaps softer ground wasn't ideal; pressed leader, edged ahead 2f out, headed final 1f, no extra final 100 yds; he may yet do better, though unlike most of these he isn't really bred to appreciate any further. **Hans Andersen** wasn't disgraced without running any better than he had in the Futurity, maybe just coming up short for ability; made running, joined 2f out, every chance still last ½f, faded. **Marbaan** proved to be a disappointment, probably just unsuited by conditions; held up, brief headway 2f out, weakened.

NEWMARKET (ROWLEY) Saturday September 24
GOOD

Juddmonte Royal Lodge Stakes (Group 2) (1)

Pos	Draw	Btn	Horse	Age	Wgt	Eq	Trainer	Jockey	SP
1	3		THE FOXES (IRE)	2	9-2		Andrew Balding	David Probert	17/2
2	2	½	DUBAI MILE (IRE)	2	9-2		Charlie & Mark Johnston	Daniel Muscutt	16/1
3	1	sh	FLYING HONOURS	2	9-2		Charlie Appleby	William Buick	2/7f
4	4	¾	GREENLAND (IRE)	2	9-2		Aidan O'Brien, Ireland	Ryan Moore	13/2

4 ran   Race Time 1m 43.66   Closing Sectional (3.00f): 33.65s (115.5%)   Winning Owner: King Power Racing Co Ltd

An unsatisfactory race, run at a dawdle and developing into a 2f sprint, not a proper test for staying 2-y-os obviously, the form suspect and best viewed cautiously, even though the quartet as individuals all had a fair bit going for them, hopefully another opportunity around the corner to offer a proper test of their merits. **The Foxes** followed the second and third from his debut race in landing a pattern event, confirming the favourable impression he'd created in that race and in his win last time, albeit this a farcical race, the 1f longer trip neither here nor there in a 2f sprint, though hopefully he will get a chance in a truer test before long, the Futurity an option next month; held up, headway 2f out, led under pressure well inside final 1f, ran on. **Dubai Mile** bidding to emulate his sire, who won this race in 2017, ran well upped in grade, though the form is clearly not the most satisfactory and he dictated, like the others entered in the Futurity, which may offer a better guide to the respective merits of the quartet; led, shaken up over 2f out, hung right, hung left, headed well inside final 1f, kept on. **Flying Honours** stood out on form, but he wasn't able to make that count in a race that developed into a 2f sprint, which didn't play to his strengths at all, every chance that he will progress again once his stamina is properly tested; tracked pace, shaken up over 2f out, every chance when bumped inside final 1f, not quicken final 100 yds; his stable has plenty of depth to its 2-y-o team, but a chance to gain compensation in the Futurity would seem a likely option for him. **Greenland** ran about as well as could have been expected upped in grade, though the nature of the race meant nothing was going to be beaten very far; in touch, travelled well, shaken up 2f out, bumped soon after, not quicken well inside final 1f.

Juddmonte Cheveley Park Stakes (Group 1) (1)

Pos	Draw	Btn	Horse	Age	Wgt	Eq	Trainer	Jockey	SP
1	6		LEZOO	2	9-2		Ralph Beckett	William Buick	11/2
2	3	¾	MEDITATE (IRE)	2	9-2		Aidan O'Brien, Ireland	Ryan Moore	13/8f
3	1	¾	MAWJ (IRE)	2	9-2		Saeed bin Suroor	Ray Dawson	10/1
4	5	2½	SWINGALONG (IRE)	2	9-2		K. R. Burke	Clifford Lee	12/1
5	2	½	JULIET SIERRA	2	9-2		Ralph Beckett	Rob Hornby	18/1
6	9	nk	TREASURE TROVE (IRE)	2	9-2		P. Twomey, Ireland	William James Lee	11/1
7	10	1¾	MAYLANDSEA	2	9-2		Michael Bell	Tom Marquand	125/1
8	7	2	TRILLIUM	2	9-2		Richard Hannon	Pat Dobbs	3/1
9	8	3¼	MALRESCIA (IRE)	2	9-2	(t)	George Boughey	Andrea Atzeni	150/1
10	4	2¼	WAVE MACHINE (FR)	2	9-2		John Patrick Murtagh, Ireland	Daniel Muscutt	150/1

10 ran Race Time 1m 11.84 Closing Sectional (3.00f): 34.90s (102.9%) Winning Owner: Marc Chan & Andrew Rosen

The Cheveley Park, the first of two Group 1s in Britain for 2-y-o fillies, featured 7 that had won pattern events already, the field clearly a representative one, and although Trillium, about the best of them beforehand, failed to give her running, the form has a solid look to it, the winner's performance roughly on a par with most recent scorers in the race, this as a contest more a summary of the merits of the 2-y-o sprinting fillies than a race offering a lot for next year, the winner with no pretensions to stay much beyond 6f and a bit lacking in scope as well, the time quicker than that for the Middle Park, the timefigure fully backing up the view of the form. **Lezoo** off 2 months (the longest absent of the whole field), found improvement again to make it 4 wins from 5 starts, a speedier type than the placed pair and making that tell, her future likely to be as a sprinter, though she lacks size and it may be that she won't be quite so good at 3 yrs, a trip to the Breeders' Cup her final target for this year; held up, travelled well, headway over 2f out, led over 1f out, ridden, quickened, had bit in hand. **Meditate** found one too good again, though ran to a similar level as last time, doing well despite rather than because of the shorter trip, probably the only plausible

Guineas candidate in the field; prominent, shaken up halfway, every chance over 1f out, left behind by winner, stuck to task. **Mawj** ran at least as well as previously, sticking to her task once the winner had gone for home, remaining worth a try at 7f; in touch, effort over 2f out, every chance over 1f out, kept on. **Swingalong** failed to make the further progress expected, unable to confirm York placings with the third, perhaps doing a bit too much in front but essentially beaten fair and square; led, took keen hold, shaken up over 2f out, headed over 1f out, not quicken, no extra late on. **Juliet Sierra** ran creditably, up in grade, no obvious excuses on the day, though with a bit more about her physically than most of these and some prospect that she will progress at 3 yrs; waited with, shaken up over 2f out, not quicken, kept on inside final 1f. **Treasure Trove** wasn't disgraced, up in grade, though she never really threatened to get involved, a useful filly but one physically that looks as if the best of her might be seen at 2 yrs; slowly into stride, held up, not settle fully, shaken up over 2f out, stayed on final 1f, never on terms. **Maylandsea** took a step forward, this easily her best effort since the Queen Mary, though hard to know whether racing solo was a disadvantage or not; raced alone stand side, close up 4f. **Trillium** ran poorly, clearly not herself, this perhaps coming too soon after Doncaster, her failure to settle and awkwardness on the track both looking factors in her defeat; held up, not settle fully, in touch after 2f, shaken up 2f out, looked ill at ease, left behind; she's clearly best judged on her earlier form. **Malrescia** ran better than last time, but was still below form, this company just too hot for her; chased leader, took keen hold, shaken up soon after halfway, weakened 2f out. **Wave Machine** was out of her depth; handy, shaken up 2f out, weakened quickly.

Juddmonte Middle Park Stakes (Group 1) (1)

Pos	Draw	Btn	Horse	Age	Wgt	Eq	Trainer	Jockey	SP
1	2		BLACKBEARD (IRE)	2	9-2		Aidan O'Brien, Ireland	Ryan Moore	10/3
2	5	2	THE ANTARCTIC (IRE)	2	9-2		Aidan O'Brien, Ireland	Tom Marquand	16/1
3	7	1¼	PERSIAN FORCE (IRE)	2	9-2		Richard Hannon	Rossa Ryan	6/1
4	8	¾	MISCHIEF MAGIC (IRE)	2	9-2		Charlie Appleby	William Buick	10/3
5	6	1	MARSHMAN	2	9-2		K. R. Burke	Clifford Lee	15/8f
6	4	2¾	ONCE MORE FOR LUCK (IRE)	2	9-2		Ismail Mohammed	Benoit de la Sayette	250/1
7	1	2¾	ZOOLOGY	2	9-2		James Ferguson	Cieren Fallon	11/1
8	3	5	NEVER JUST A DREAM (IRE)	2	9-2		Ismail Mohammed	Cameron Noble	80/1

8 ran Race Time 1m 12.02 Closing Sectional (3.00f): 36.10s (99.8%) Winning Owner: D.Smith,Mrs J.Magnier,M.Tabor,Westerberg

A Middle Park lacking the 2 best sprinting 2-y-o colts of the campaign, Little Big Bear and the Gimcrack winner Noble Style, the latter's form represented by the runner-up at York Marshman, though he failed to give his running, the finish contested by a trio that had been on the go since very early in the season, the winner having his sixth start in a pattern event, the placed horses their fifth, the merit of the trio pretty well established, though the winner clearly progressed again, standing up really well to such a busy campaign. **Blackbeard** proved better than ever in gaining a third successive win in pattern company, clearly thriving on racing, signs of his usual quirks beforehand but none once racing, some elements of his pedigree offering hope that he would stay 7f or even 1m (entered in the Irish Guineas), though sprinting more likely to be his aim at 3 yrs, a run at the Breeders' Cup a final task for his juvenile campaign; waited with, travelled well, shaken up over 2f out, led over 1f out, kept on well. **The Antarctic** produced a career best, though for the third time he was in the wake of his stable companion, helped by a good pace and doing his best work late on; slowly into stride, held up, shaken up after halfway, stayed on approaching final 1f, took second last ½f; likely the winner he's thrived on a busy campaign, whether he can bridge the gap to pattern winner at 3 yrs remaining to be seen, sprinting clearly likely to be his role. **Persian Force** ran creditably, placed now in all 5 pattern events he's contested, though successful just once, here if anything doing a bit too much in front, which may have cost him second; close up, went with zest, led after 2f, ridden over 2f out, headed over 1f out, not quicken, edged right; he's a useful colt and one that has stood up to a busy campaign well, but it may be that the best of him has been seen this year. **Mischief Magic** wasn't discredited but found a further rise in grade beyond him, back on turf and on the easiest ground he's faced, his turn of foot lacking in this stronger race; held up, travelled well, effort over 2f out, plugged on, made little impression. **Marshman** looked to hold leading form claims and disappointed, largely due to his headstrong ways, though he didn't seem entirely at home on the track under pressure either, the ground also the softest he will have encountered; prominent, refused to settle, ridden over 2f out, edged right, not quicken, no extra over 1f out. **Once More For Luck** wasted no time getting back to form, doing well, given the stiffness of the task he faced; in touch, pushed along halfway, not quicken 2f out, no extra inside final 1f. **Zoology** had looked an exciting prospect in winning at Yarmouth but tackling a Group 1 just 11 days on proved much more than he could cope with, given a harder race than perhaps ideal; held up, ridden over 2f out, ran green, not quicken, dropped away over 1f out; may yet do better. **Never Just A Dream** was simply out of his depth, though there's also a chance that he's better on all-weather; led 2f, remained prominent, weakened 2f out.

LONGCHAMP Sunday October 2
Soft

Qatar Prix Jean-Luc Lagardere (Grand Criterium) (Group 1) (Colts And Fillies)

Pos	Draw	Btn	Horse	Age	Wgt	Eq	Trainer	Jockey	SP
1	3		BELBEK (FR)	2	9-0		A. Fabre, France	Mickael Barzalona	18/1
2	1	nk	GAMESTOP (IRE)	2	9-0	(h)	Christophe Ferland, France	Maxime Guyon	12/1
3	4	nk	BREIZH SKY (FR)	2	9-0		A. & G. Botti, France	Christophe Soumillon	38/10
4	2	2	SHARTASH (IRE)	2	9-0		John Patrick Murtagh, Ireland	Ben Martin Coen	1/1f
5	8	ns	VICIOUS HARRY (FR)	2	9-0		M. Delcher Sanchez, France	Tony Piccone	13/1
6	6	3	TIGRAIS (FR)	2	8-11		Christopher Head, France	Aurelien Lemaitre	4/1
7	5	1	PIVOTAL TRIGGER	2	9-0		Mrs J. Harrington, Ireland	Shane Foley	9/1

7 ran   Race Time 1m 22.98   Winning Owner: Mr Nurlan Bizakov

The 2 Irish raiders formed the full extent of the raiding party but neither Pivotal Trigger nor the standard-setting Shartash were at their best and the home contingent swept the places, Belbek finishing well to edge it in the final 50 yds, the fairly bunched finish meaning the form looks no more than average for a race with a mixed overall record of producing high-class 3-y-os. **Belbek** put up a smart effort to cause a minor surprise, stepping up in trip the obvious catalyst; in touch, chased leaders over 1f out, stayed on to lead near finish; he'll have no trouble staying 1m and the Futurity at Doncaster was mentioned as an option, though he'd have to be supplemented and that race typically takes more winning than this one. **Gamestop** improved under a more forward ride and in a first-time hood, reversing form with the 2 that had beaten him in the Prix La Rochette here a month earlier; prominent, led under 2f out, collared near finish; there's stamina in his pedigree to think he'll have little trouble stay at least 1m. **Breizh Sky** produced his best effort to date, finishing well from out the back; dropped out, travelled well, headway when switched 1f out, ran on; he'll stay 1m and is clearly up to winning some good races. **Shartash** wasn't in the same form as in the National Stakes, not really picking up, 3 weeks perhaps not enough time to recover from that good run on heavy ground; held up, effort out wide under 2f out, not quicken. **Vicious Harry** ran well on form, not caving in once headed and clearly effective at the new trip; soon led, headed under 2f out, one paced. **Tigrais** wasn't in the same form as last time, when she'd beaten both the second and third, softer ground and an early stumble perhaps reasons why; propped leaving stalls, held up, brief headway under 2f out, faded. **Pivotal Trigger** wasn't in the same form as last time; prominent, ridden 2f out, faded.

Qatar Prix Marcel Boussac - Criterium des Pouliches (Group 1) (Fillies)

Pos	Draw	Btn	Horse	Age	Wgt	Eq	Trainer	Jockey	SP
1	5		BLUE ROSE CEN (IRE)	2	8-11		Christopher Head, France	Aurelien Lemaitre	47/10
2	1	5	GAN TEORAINN (IRE)	2	8-11	(b)	J. S. Bolger, Ireland	K. J. Manning	50/1
3	2	sn	NEVER ENDING STORY (IRE)	2	8-11		Aidan O'Brien, Ireland	Ryan Moore	67/10
4	8	sn	START ME UP (FR)	2	8-11		P. Decouz, France	Stephane Pasquier	30/1
5	9	1¼	BREEGE	2	8-11		John Quinn	Jason Hart	25/1
6	10	nk	ARDENT (USA)	2	8-11		A. Fabre, France	Mickael Barzalona	66/10
7	6	nk	ASPEN GROVE (IRE)	2	8-11		J. A. Stack, Ireland	Jamie Spencer	35/1
8	11	nk	SHALROMY (FR)	2	8-11		Christophe Ferland, France	Christophe Soumillon	21/1
9	4	1	DANDY ALYS (IRE)	2	8-11		Ralph Beckett	Rob Hornby	30/1
10	12	4½	WED (FR)	2	8-11		Maurizio Guarnieri, France	Cristian Demuro	76/10
11	3	hd	HABANA (GER)	2	8-11		Andreas Wohler, Germany	Eduardo Pedroza	72/10
12	7	6½	KELINA (IRE)	2	8-11		C. Laffon-Parias, France	Maxime Guyon	21/10f

12 ran Race Time 1m 40.45 Winning Owner: Yeguada Centurion Slu

Not a field beforehand that looked likely to produce a winner worthy of France's top race for two-year-old fillies but Blue Rose Cen is thriving and showed plenty of improvement to deliver a smart performance, drawing right away in the final furlong after the pace set by Shalromy and Ardent made this a good test in the conditions, outsider Gan Teorainn another suited by the test of stamina in second; the winner bucked a notable trend in becoming the first Prix d'Aumale winner since Mary Linoa in 1988 to follow up in this contest and has another stat to overcome as none of the last 4 Marcel Boussac winners has managed to win a race the following season. **Blue Rose Cen** has generally been on an upward curve but this was much improved form, the combination of a well-run race and soft ground evidently something she relished; tracked pace, switched to the rail at the cutaway over 2f out, quickened to lead over 1f out, drew clear final 1f, suited by emphasis on stamina; she's clearly smart, beaten only by the Ballydoyle colt Victoria Road in her last four starts, and, out of a mare who ended up winning at Grade 3 level in the States over 1½m, she'll stay longer trips next year. **Gan Teorainn** was the rank outsider but after just 7 days off showed improved form, as expected suited by the return to 1m for the first time since winning her maiden on her only previous try at the trip; mid-division, squeezed through on rail before stayed on to claim second close home, suited by emphasis on stamina; like the winner, she'll be suited by further next year. **Never Ending Story** upped in trip, had more of a chance to show what she could do this time and was back to her best; held up, headway when switched over 1f out, kept on into second in the final 1f before losing that spot close home; like the pair who beat her, her pedigree suggests she'll stay at least another couple of furlongs next year. **Start Me Up**, third to Blue Rose Cen in the Prix d'Aumale, ran creditably without showing the same improvement as the winner from that race; held up, didn't get the smoothest of runs in the straight, ran on late. **Breege** upped in trip/on softer ground than previously didn't fail for a lack of stamina, running just about her best race yet in fact; held up, progress home turn, kept on final 1f, never landed a blow. **Ardent** (by Frankel; sister to winner up to 1½m (including over 7.5f/1m at 2 yrs) Raclette and 9.5f winner Licence, both useful, and half-sister to 2-y-o 6f winner Peace Charter (by War Front): dam, Emollient, US Grade 1 8.5f-1¼m winner) up markedly in grade, showed improved form but paid for racing close to the pace; pressed leader, travelled well, challenged over 2f out, disputing second 1f out before no extra final 1f, did too much too soon; she was third in a newcomers race at Deauville behind Kelina and Shalromy (both behind her here) before winning a minor event at Saint-Cloud last month and is bred to be suited by at least 1¼m next year. **Aspen Grove** ran to a similar level as when pulling off a shock last time but never looked like getting involved; in rear, still last 1f out before passing beaten horses. **Dandy Alys** ran as well as could be expected up in grade but shaped as though this longer trip stretched her stamina; mid-division, in a challenging position 2f out, weakened out of it final 1f.

NEWMARKET (ROWLEY) Friday October 7
GOOD

Bet365 Fillies' Mile (Group 1) (1)

Pos	Draw	Btn	Horse	Age	Wgt	Eq	Trainer	Jockey	SP
1	4		COMMISSIONING	2	9-2	(h)	John & Thady Gosden	Robert Havlin	8/13f
2	3	1	NOVAKAI	2	9-2		K. R. Burke	William Buick	11/1
3	1	4¾	BRIGHT DIAMOND (IRE)	2	9-2		K. R. Burke	Clifford Lee	7/1
4	8	1¼	POLLY POTT	2	9-2		Harry Dunlop	David Probert	14/1
5	7	¾	LIBRARY (IRE)	2	9-2		Aidan O'Brien, Ireland	Ryan Moore	7/1
6	6	2	SPARKLING BEAUTY (FR)	2	9-2		Richard Hughes	David Egan	12/1
7	2	5½	ALSEYOOB (IRE)	2	9-2		Ismail Mohammed	Tom Marquand	40/1
8	5	¾	FERRARI QUEEN (IRE)	2	9-2		Charlie & Mark Johnston	Andrea Atzeni	28/1

8 ran Race Time 1m 36.53 Closing Sectional (3.00f): 35.70s (101.4%) Winning Owner: Isa Salman & Abdulla Al Khalifa

The Rockfel Stakes winner Commissioning stood out on form and was sent off at odds on in the premier race for staying 2-y-o fillies, most of the rest having a fair bit to find to be involved in an average running, including the first 2 from the May Hill and fillies placed in the Prestige Stakes and the Prix du Calvados, that the favourite had to work harder than expected to prevail initially seeming a bit disappointing, but probably better to credit the runner-up with improved form under a well-judged ride, the first 2 pulling well clear; Commissioning gave John Gosden his sixth win in the race, worth noting that the last 3, Inspiral, Rainbow View and Nannina went on to at least one Group 1 win subsequently, the first 2, Playful Act and Crystal Music placed in a classic; the field raced as 2 groups of 4 initially, that the first 3 came from the group next to the rail something to bear in mind, rather than to think it was significant. **Commissioning** stood out on form and didn't need to improve to maintain her unbeaten record, stepped up to 1m, taking time to find full stride, this not visually so impressive as her win in the Rockfel, though the runner-up deserves credit for that, and this came just 2 weeks on, which might have been a little quick, a path to the classics still very much on the agenda; tracked pace, travelled well, shaken up 2f out, not quicken, challenged inside final 1f, led final 100 yds, had bit in hand; likely to progress further and a leading contender for classic honours in 2023. **Novakai** showed much improved form on her third try at pattern level, suited by a positive ride that placed the emphasis firmly on stamina; led, went with zest, shaken up over 2f out, kept on well, headed final 100 yds, not quicken; she's likely to prove effective at middle distances next year, her performance here good enough to encourage a run in a trial of some description in the spring. **Bright Diamond** progressed again over 1f longer trip, even if no threat to the principals, shaping as if the trip suited her, even though she was on her toes beforehand; tracked pace, ridden soon after halfway, not quicken, plugged on final 1f. **Polly Pott** had her winning sequence ended, tackling the highest grade, just not in the same form as last time, the runner-up turning the tables comprehensively and the better prospect of the 2; held up, effort over 2f out, outpaced over 1f out, plugged on final 1f, never on terms. **Library** something of a token runner for a yard with such a good record in the race, ran about as well as could have been expected upped in grade; prominent, shaken up 3f out, one paced; she's bred to stay middle distances and could step up again next year. **Sparkling Beauty** wasn't in the same form as last time, possibly partly due to not seeing out the extra 1f; patiently ridden, travelled well, headway over 3f out, shaken up over 2f out, edged right, not quicken, no extra inside final 1f. **Alseyoob** had a lot to find on form and just looked out of her depth; held up, shaken up 3f out, made no impression. **Ferrari Queen** was well held, facing her stiffest task to date; prominent, shaken up over 3f out, lost place soon after.

NEWMARKET (ROWLEY) Saturday October 8
GOOD

Emirates Autumn Stakes (Group 3) (1)

Pos	Draw	Btn	Horse	Age	Wgt	Eq	Trainer	Jockey	SP
1	3		SILVER KNOTT	2	9-6		Charlie Appleby	William Buick	4/1
2	1	nk	EPICTETUS (IRE)	2	9-3		John & Thady Gosden	Frankie Dettori	9/4
3	6	1¾	HOLLOWAY BOY	2	9-3		K. R. Burke	Clifford Lee	2/1f
4	5	¾	DANCING MAGIC (IRE)	2	9-3		Roger Teal	Jim Crowley	20/1
5	2	4	KILLYBEGS WARRIOR (IRE)	2	9-3		Charlie & Mark Johnston	Andrea Atzeni	28/1
6	4	5½	EXOPLANET (FR)	2	9-3		Roger Varian	David Egan	5/1

6 ran Race Time 1m 36.00 Closing Sectional (3.00f): 35.10s (102.6%) Winning Owner: Godolphin

As with the Zetland Stakes, this race provided an opportunity to get back on track for an Appleby-trained runner beaten at odds on last time, Silver Knott giving his yard a fourth win in the race since 2017 and a third in a row, Ghaiyyath and Coroebus 2 of the other 3, his form on a par with theirs in winning this, even if he doesn't have quite the obvious potential the latter showed when successful in 2021, if anything the runner-up the more exciting prospect for next year, experience more than ability tipping the balance late on in a race run at a sound gallop. **Silver Knott** clearly hadn't done himself justice when odds on for the Champagne Stakes and got back on the up in gaining a second victory at this level, looking well suited by the step up to 1m, this trip likely to be a bare minimum for him at 3 yrs, though it seems likely he'll start off aimed at the Guineas, a trip to the Breeders' Cup on the cards before that; tracked pace, effort over 2f out, stayed on to lead inside last ½f. **Epictetus** coincidentally had had 2 other winners on this card, Flying Honours and Desert Order, behind him when winning on debut, and although he couldn't himself add a second victory, he acquitted himself really well after 3 months off, if anything a better prospect than the winner, his lack of experience just finding him out late on; tracked pace, shaken up over 2f out, led over 1f out, headed inside last ½f; a smart prospect, sure to win a good race or 2 at 3 yrs. **Holloway Boy** looked suited by the extra 1f, but just lacked pace at a crucial stage and could run no better than he had on his last 2 starts, a bit short of room against the stand rail at times but third best regardless; handy, shaken up 3f out, not quicken, stayed on inside final 1f; he'll stay 1¼m. **Dancing Magic** seemed to excel himself, up still further in grade, the pace he set good enough to think that he wasn't flattered in making the running, his pedigree promising still more to come when he goes over middle distances; led, ridden over 2f out, headed over 1f out, no extra well inside final 1f. **Killybegs Warrior** had plenty on at this level and ran about as well as could be expected, class telling as he dropped away late on, very likely to be fully effective at the trip in the right grade; close up, shaken up 3f out, weakened over 1f out. **Exoplanet** attracted support, fast-tracked to pattern company after his debut win, that form having been boosted since, though he failed to enhance it himself, just too short on experience to make an impact; slowly into stride, held up, shaken up over 2f out, left behind soon after; he's an excellent middle-distance pedigree and is well worth another chance to progress.

Darley Dewhurst Stakes (Group 1) (1)

Pos	Draw	Btn	Horse	Age	Wgt	Eq	Trainer	Jockey	SP
1	5		CHALDEAN	2	9-3		Andrew Balding	Frankie Dettori	5/2jf
2	7	hd	ROYAL SCOTSMAN (IRE)	2	9-3		Paul & Oliver Cole	Jim Crowley	12/1
3	3	2¼	NOSTRUM	2	9-3		Sir Michael Stoute	Richard Kingscote	5/2jf
4	4	5	AESOP'S FABLES (IRE)	2	9-3		Aidan O'Brien, Ireland	Ryan Moore	5/1
5	2	1	MARBAAN	2	9-3		Charlie Fellowes	Jamie Spencer	25/1
6	6	3¼	NAVAL POWER	2	9-3		Charlie Appleby	William Buick	4/1
7	1	hd	ISAAC SHELBY	2	9-3		Brian Meehan	Sean Levey	14/1

7 ran   Race Time 1m 22.54   Closing Sectional (3.00f): 34.45s (102.7%)   Winning Owner: Juddmonte

In the absence of Little Big Bear and the supplemented-then-withdrawn Mill Reef winner Sakheer, a more open renewal of what is often the most significant 2-y-o race of the campaign, 6 of the previous 7 favourites having been sent off at evens or shorter, 5 of those winning, 4 of them coming into the race with a Timeform rating already at 120 or above, none in this field close to that beforehand, the winner, though improved, probably just shy of that level still, though in what isn't overall a vintage crop he ranks among the more plausible Guineas candidates, uncomplicated and with a willing attitude. **Chaldean** has developed well physically and progressed his form all season, producing his best effort yet in completing a 4-timer, a willing attitude and uncomplicated style again on show;

soon led, shaken up under 3f out, kept on well final 1f, ridden out; he has the Guineas as the obvious aim in the spring, with speed on his dam's side but by Frankel, his manner suggesting he's sure to stay 1m, his form not quite at the level usually required for the classic, though he's still among the most likely of his generation for the race. **Royal Scotsman** evidently hadn't done himself justice when well fancied for the Gimcrack and resumed progress, looking well suited by the step up to 7f, likely to be at least as effective at 1m too, a Guineas presumably on the agenda in the spring; broke well, soon steadied, travelled well, effort 2f out, chased leader entering final 1f, kept on well. **Nostrum** had looked such an exciting prospect in winning his first 2 starts, and though that bubble was burst, he's such a good looker with a fine pedigree and in a top yard, that he'll surely resume his progress in the spring; tracked pace, took keen hold, shaken up over 2f out, not quicken approaching final 1f, faded late on. **Aesop's Fables** looked in fine shape, but failed to meet expectations again, no excuse with the ground this time, something to prove when he's next seen; held up, shaken up under 3f out, not quicken, left behind over 1f out. **Marbaan** again failed to repeat the form shown in winning the Vintage Stakes, that looking very solid, below par twice since, no excuse with the ground on this occasion, a bit to prove when next seen; steadied at the start, in rear, ridden over 2f out, not quicken, plugged on final 1f. **Naval Power** attracted support, up in grade, his stable's selected from a deep team and with 2 wins in the race in the last 3 years, but he failed to give his running and proved to be amiss; close up, took keen hold, shaken up 3f out, soon beaten, reportedly bled; he'll be best judged on his earlier form when he returns, presumably next year. **Isaac Shelby** was below form after 3 months off, the form of his Superlative Stakes win looking suspect now and his stable without a winner in over 2 months; slowly into stride, in touch, shaken up 3f out, not quicken, weakened over 1f out.

DONCASTER Saturday October 22
HEAVY

Vertem Futurity Trophy Stakes (Group 1) (1)

Pos	Draw	Btn	Horse	Age	Wgt	Eq	Trainer	Jockey	SP
1	6		AUGUSTE RODIN (IRE)	2	9-3		Aidan O'Brien, Ireland	Ryan Moore	9/4f
2	7	3½	EPICTETUS (IRE)	2	9-3		John & Thady Gosden	Frankie Dettori	3/1
3	5	1¾	HOLLOWAY BOY	2	9-3	(v)	K. R. Burke	Daniel Tudhope	9/2
4	3	3¾	DANCING MAGIC (IRE)	2	9-3		Roger Teal	Jim Crowley	14/1
5	8	nk	SALT LAKE CITY (IRE)	2	9-3		Aidan O'Brien, Ireland	W. M. Lordan	7/1
6	1	sh	CAPTAIN WIERZBA	2	9-3		Ralph Beckett	Rob Hornby	40/1
7	2	nk	KING OF STEEL (USA)	2	9-3		David Loughnane	Adam Kirby	12/1
8	4	2	STORMBUSTER	2	9-3		Andrew Balding	David Probert	7/1

8 ran Race Time 1m 44.76 Closing Sectional (2.00f): 28.45s (92.1%) Winning Owner: M Tabor/D Smith/Mrs J Magnier/Westerberg

Although the race unfolded in unorthodox fashion, the field splitting into 2 groups with the 3 highest drawn sticking to the stand rail and the rest coming down the centre, the latter group pressing on too far out, Auguste Rodin is still worth crediting with another significant step forward as he ran out an authoritative winner, giving Aidan O'Brien an eleventh success in the race, the frame filled by those who had been placed in lesser pattern events earlier in the season; like other races on the card, conditions played their part in ensuring a thorough test of stamina. **Auguste Rodin** hasn't looked back as he's gone through the grades since his unlucky debut defeat, putting up a very smart effort 6 weeks on from Leopardstown to run out a comfortable winner; patiently ridden, smooth headway from 3f out, ridden 2f out, led 1f out, forged clear; he's bred along very similar lines to the 2017 winner of this, Saxon Warrior, by Deep Impact out of a Galileo mare, who went on to win the Guineas the following spring, Auguste Rodin convincing as the best classic prospect the yard has over the winter, even if his form lags a shade behind his stablemate Little Big Bear at this stage, though the Guineas will ask different questions of him, very likely to be much more of a speed test than here, and it's not the biggest surprise that he's a shorter price for the Derby than the opening classic, every chance of staying 1½m on pedigree. **Epictetus** has come a long way in little time, this a second start in pattern company just a fortnight on from the Autumn Stakes and he ran to a similar level here as he again found only one too good, no doubting that he's a smart juvenile; mid-field, ridden over 2f out, forced to switch inside final 1f, plugged on; though by Kingman, his dam was a Group 1 winner over a mile and quarter and this colt should stay that far next year. **Holloway Boy** might have been a big price when winning the Chesham, but he's backed it up time and time again in pattern company since and ran well on form in a first-time visor, things perhaps not panning out ideally for him as he raced on the far side initially; held up, tanked along, led over 2f out, hung badly right to join other group, headed 1f out, weakened; he ended up having a hard race and is probably done for the year now and though he's not far off smart, it remains to be seen if he can take his form any higher in 2023. **Dancing Magic** had seemed to have his limitations exposed in the Autumn Stakes and did so again in this even better race; chased leader, pushed along 3f out, weakened inside final 1f. **Salt Lake City** didn't have the chance the market suggested coming here on the back of just a maiden win and he matched his previous form, doing his job to ensure his stablemate got a good tow into the race; led group, headed 2f out, weakened. **Captain Wierzba** had something to find stepping into top company and ran as well as could be expected; held up, pushed along over 3f out, never involved. **King of Steel** had looked a good prospect when winning his maiden just 10 days ago and though advancing his form, looked out of his depth at this stage of his career; awkward leaving stalls, mid-field, pushed along soon after halfway, weakened over 2f out; he's a grand sort physically and remains with longer-term potential. **Stormbuster** was below form up in grade on softer ground than previously, having too much use made of him; led group, ridden under 3f out, headed over 2f out, hung left, weakened inside final 1f.

BEST OF 2022 IN EUROPE

Juveniles

Aidan O'Brien gained an incredible seventeenth success in the Phoenix Stakes at the Curragh and **Little Big Bear** (126p) was arguably as impressive as any of his previous winners, powering clear in the final furlong to beat the July Stakes winner **Persian Force** (108) by seven lengths. That victory was his fourth in a row since being turned over on his debut and it was just a shame that he missed the rest of the season due to injury. Still, Little Big Bear proved himself to be a high-class juvenile—he achieved the highest Timeform rating of any two-year-old in Europe in 2022—and he is unsurprisingly at the head of the ante-post betting for the 2000 Guineas.

Blackbeard (118) capitalised on his stablemate's absence by claiming back-to-back Group 1 wins in the second half of the campaign, first winning the Prix Morny at Deauville and then taking his form up another notch to follow up in the Middle Park Stakes at Newmarket (by two lengths from **The Antarctic** (111)). Blackbeard won six of his eight starts all told, but he won't get the opportunity to add to his tally as he

Little Big Bear powers clear of his rivals in the Phoenix Stakes

was retired to stud having suffered a setback when being prepared for a run at the Breeders' Cup. Regardless, Ballydoyle won't lack for exciting three-year-olds in 2023 and **Auguste Rodin** (121p) looks another serious classic prospect for the stable having run out an emphatic winner of the Futurity Trophy at Doncaster, asserting late on to beat **Epictetus** (111) by three and a half lengths. He's a shorter price for the Derby than he is the opening classic, with every chance of him staying a mile and a half on pedigree.

The first three from the Dewhurst Stakes at Newmarket are all likely to be aimed at the Guineas, certainly the progressive winner **Chaldean** (118), who typically showed a willing attitude to get the verdict by a head from the Richmond Stakes winner **Royal Scotsman** (118), with another two and a quarter lengths back to **Nostrum** (112p) in third. A notable absentee was the wide-margin Mill Reef Stakes winner **Sakheer** (115p), who had been supplemented a few days earlier but was forced to miss the race due to a dirty scope.

Earlier on that card, the Charlie Appleby-trained **Silver Knott** (115) showed smart form to give 3 lb and a neck-beating to Epictetus in the Autumn Stakes. Silver Knott went on to suffer a short-head defeat in the Breeders' Cup Juvenile Turf at Keeneland, losing out on the nod to O'Brien's **Victoria Road** (114p), but Appleby was already on the scoreboard at that meeting by then having saddled **Mischief Magic** (113) to win the Breeders' Cup Juvenile Turf Sprint. Incidentally, it's a sign of the strength in depth that Appleby had in this division that neither Silver Knott nor Mischief Magic was his highest-rated two-year-old, with that honour instead belonging to the unbeaten **Noble Style** (119p), who made it three from three when beating **Marshman** (114) by a length and a quarter in the Gimcrack Stakes at York.

Coventry Stakes winner **Bradsell** (113)—who suffered a season-ending injury when down the field behind Little Big Bear in the Phoenix—and National Stakes winner **Al Riffa** (114p) also deserve a special mention. Bradsell had the likes of Persian Force, Royal Scotsman and Blackbeard behind him when winning the Coventry, while the form of the National Stakes also received a significant boost when the runner-up, **Proud And Regal** (110), won the Criterium International at Saint-Cloud. Galileo has now sired 97 individual Group/Grade 1 winners after that win for Proud And Regal, while another notable milestone was achieved on the same card when **Dubai Mile** (112) won the Criterium de Saint-Cloud, providing his sire Roaring Lion with a Group 1 winner in his first and only crop.

Also in France, **Belbek** (111) won the Prix Jean-Luc Lagardere and **Blue Rose Cen** (114) won the Prix Marcel Boussac, the two Group 1 races restricted to juveniles on the Arc undercard at Longchamp, while the Prix de l'Abbaye on the same afternoon was also won by a two-year-old for the first time since 1978, namely the speedy filly **The Platinum Queen** (111). However, top billing among the two-year-old fillies in

Europe went the way of **Tahiyra** (116P), who looked potentially something out of the ordinary when dismissing the subsequent Breeders' Cup Juvenile Fillies Turf winner **Meditate** (114) in the Moyglare Stud Stakes at the Curragh by two and a quarter lengths. Tahiyra was ranked comfortably ahead of the likes of **Commissioning** (112p), the unbeaten winner of the Fillies' Mile at Newmarket—who has since been retired due to injury—and **Lezoo** (112), who also had Meditate behind her when winning the Cheveley Park Stakes at Newmarket.

Sprinters

One sprinter put up a performance last season that was head and shoulders above the others in this division, at least on European soil. Even then, it was the Australian-trained **Nature Strip** (131) who came up with it as he registered a breathtaking victory in the King's Stand Stakes at Royal Ascot, leaving his rivals for dead over a furlong out and ultimately winning by four and a half lengths from **Twilight Calls** (117). Nature Strip's connections then declined the opportunity to try and emulate Blue Point by following up in the Platinum Jubilee Stakes later in the week, a decision they might have been left to rue given how that race developed. Nature Strip's stablemate **Home Affairs** (128) ended up finishing well down the field and the winner, **Naval Crown** (121?), needed

Nature Strip was an emphatic winner of the King's Stand Stakes

to show just very smart form to come out on top in a bunched finish (the first 11 runners past the post were covered by less than three lengths).

Naval Crown made his next appearance in the July Cup at Newmarket where many of his closest pursuers from Royal Ascot were in opposition once again. They included stablemate **Creative Force** (120), who had filled the runner-up spot in the Platinum Jubilee, and the Australian raider **Artorius** (119), who had dead-heated for third with the US-trained **Campanelle** (116). In the event, however, it was the ninth-place finisher in the Platinum Jubilee, **Alcohol Free** (123), who ran out a decisive winner of the July Cup, gaining the fourth Group 1 success of her career as she asserted inside the final furlong to beat Naval Crown by a length and a half.

The first six in the July Cup were all older horses and it was certainly a race in which the form of the three-year-olds took a big knock, with **Perfect Power** (119) and **Flaming Rib** (115), the first two from the Commonwealth Cup, both finishing down the field. Flaming Rib made a bold bid at Royal Ascot as he tried to go one better than when chasing home **El Caballo** (116) in the Sandy Lane Stakes at Haydock on his previous start, but he once again found one too good as Perfect Power ran out a clear-cut winner, registering his third Group 1 victory in the process having also won the Prix Morny and Middle Park Stakes at two. At that stage Perfect Power looked set for a productive summer at the highest level, but he met with defeat in all three starts against his elders, following his July Cup run with underwhelming displays in the Prix Maurice de Gheest at Deauville and Champions Sprint Stakes at Ascot.

The Prix Maurice de Gheest was won by **Highfield Princess** (126), who didn't look back after finishing a close-up sixth in the Platinum Jubilee, laying down a serious claim for the title of Europe's leading sprinter with three straight Group 1 wins. She made every yard of the running to win at Deauville, ultimately beating **Minzaal** (127) by three quarters of a length, before taking the drop back to five furlongs in her stride with a smooth two-and-a-half-length success in the Nunthorpe Stakes at York. Just as impressive when also winning the Flying Five Stakes at the Curragh, by three and a quarter lengths, Highfield Princess is a credit to her connections and her return to action in 2023 is eagerly anticipated.

Minzaal's racing days are now behind him after he was retired to stud, but he went out as a Group 1 winner having shown high-class form on his final start to win the Sprint Cup at Haydock in impressive fashion, forging clear in the final furlong to land the spoils by three and three-quarter lengths from the previous year's winner **Emaraaty Ana** (118), who just edged out **Rohaan** (121) for the runner-up spot. Rohaan had previously shown very smart form to defy a lofty mark in the Wokingham Stakes at Royal Ascot for the second year in succession, while another of the season's major sprint handicaps, the Stewards' Cup at Goodwood, also had a back-to-back winner in the shape of **Commanche Falls** (119). Rohaan was last seen finishing fourth

Baaeed is in a different league to the rest in the Lockinge Stakes

in the Champions Sprint, passing the post three lengths behind **Kinross** (123), who was winning his second Group 1 win in a row having also struck in the Prix de la Foret at Longchamp.

The three-year-old filly **Tenebrism** (117) was fifth in both the Prix de la Foret and Champions Sprint, mixing trips and producing her best effort when winning the Prix Jean Prat at Deauville. She wasn't the best of the three-year-olds in this division, though, with that honour instead belonging to the progressive **Manaccan** (122), a Group 3 winner at Dundalk on his final start of the campaign. Other members of the classic generation who deserve a mention include **Sense of Duty** (121), who was sidelined by injury after winning the Chipchase Stakes at Newcastle in good style, and **Mitbaahy** (118), who bounced back from a below-par effort behind **Khaadem** (118) in the King George Stakes at Goodwood to win the World Trophy at Newbury.

Milers

Timeform's highest-rated Flat horse in Europe, **Baaeed** (137), produced his best performance on the figures when going beyond a mile for the first time in the Juddmonte International at York, but he'd already swept aside everything in this division by then as he kicked off the campaign with top-level victories in the Lockinge Stakes at Newbury, Queen Anne Stakes at Royal Ascot and Sussex Stakes at Goodwood. Having also struck in the Prix du Moulin de Longchamp and Queen Elizabeth II Stakes at Ascot the previous year, Baaeed won a total of five Group 1 races over a mile in his illustrious career, with his Lockinge win standing out as particularly strong form, a race he won by three and a quarter lengths from **Real World** (125) despite leaving the impression he was just going through the motions after being produced to lead over a furlong out.

Baaeed stepping up in trip left this division wide open heading into the autumn and **Coroebus** (127) looked perhaps the most likely to capitalise having previously won the 2000 Guineas in taking style, showing form there which identified him as the highest-rated three-year-old miler. He looked a top-class performer in the making at Newmarket, displaying an immediate turn of foot to land the spoils by three quarters of a length from stablemate **Native Trail** (125), who went on to win the Irish 2000 Guineas at the Curragh before finishing a close-up third in the Eclipse at Sandown. Coroebus didn't run to anything like the same level when he then scrambled home in the St James's Palace Stakes at Royal Ascot, though, and he met a tragic end when suffering a fatal fall in the Prix du Moulin de Longchamp won by **Dreamloper** (123).

Maljoom (121p) was arguably an unlucky loser when forfeiting his unbeaten record in the St James's Palace having met trouble on the rail just as those around him were starting to hit top gear. He again showed a very good turn of foot once finally seeing some daylight, but the damage had already been done and he had to settle for fourth (beaten a head, a short head and a neck). Very much the type to go on improving, Maljoom subsequently missed the Prix Jacques le Marois at Deauville due to a dirty scope and wasn't seen out again during the latest season.

The Prix Jacques le Marois was won by the very smart three-year-old filly **Inspiral** (124), who found plenty to get the verdict by a neck from **Light Infantry** (122), with the same distance back to **Erevann** (122) in third. Inspiral had previously shown even better form when making a successful return to action in the Coronation Stakes at Royal Ascot, quickening clear late on to win by four and three-quarter lengths, but it wasn't all rosy for her as she also suffered a couple of expensive defeats. She was notably beaten at 7/1-on in the Falmouth Stakes at Newmarket, having to settle for the runner-up spot behind **Prosperous Voyage** (116), and sixth was the best she could muster when **Bayside Boy** (123) sprang a 33/1 surprise in the Queen Elizabeth II Stakes at Ascot.

Modern Games (122) edged out the dual Group 2 winner **Jadoomi** (119) to snatch second behind Bayside Boy at Ascot, though his best form came in North America where he won the Woodbine Mile by five and a quarter lengths and the Breeders' Cup Mile at Keeneland by three quarters of a length. He also won the Poule d'Essai des Poulains at Longchamp on his first start of the campaign and that helped Charlie Appleby to make history by becoming the first trainer to win the English, French and Irish 2000 Guineas in the same season with three different colts, the others being the Newmarket scorer Coroebus and the Curragh winner Native Trail. As for the fillies' classics, **Cachet** (113) showed a willing attitude but nothing out of the ordinary in pure form terms to win the 1000 Guineas at Newmarket, while **Mangoustine** (111) also had her limitations rather exposed after edging out Cachet to win the Poule d'Essai des Pouliches at Longchamp.

Homeless Songs (123) looked potentially a filly out of the very top drawer when she won the Irish 1000 Guineas at the Curragh by five and a half lengths, but she then failed to match that effort when down the field in both the Matron Stakes at Leopardstown won by **Pearls Galore** (121) and the Sun Chariot Stakes at Newmarket won by **Fonteyn** (119). **Saffron Beach** (121), who had previously won the Prix Rothschild at Deauville before filling the runner-up spot in the Matron, was another notable disappointment in the Sun Chariot, leaving the unexposed **Laurel** (117p) to emerge as the best of the rest on just her third start after a couple of novice wins on the all-weather at Kempton. Laurel is open to further improvement and looks sure to win good races as a four-year-old.

Middle-distances

Baaeed was tried beyond a mile for the first time in his career in the Juddmonte International at York and that provided him with the perfect platform to improve even further on the very high level of form he'd been showing, taking his record to 10 from 10 with an emphatic display. He cruised through a well-run contest and found a decisive turn of foot to leave the previous year's winner, **Mishriff** (127), trailing in his wake, ultimately winning by six and a half lengths. That performance—backed up by the timefigure—identified Baaeed as the best Flat horse trained in Europe since the days of Frankel and it was just a shame that he couldn't emulate that horse by ending his career unbeaten with victory in the Champion Stakes at Ascot. He was sent off the 4/1-on favourite on the last occasion but ultimately had to settle for fourth, just seeming a bit flat back on softer ground and never really threatening to get on terms having been caught further back than the three who beat him.

The Champion Stakes was won by **Bay Bridge** (129), who returned from four months on the sidelines with a career-best effort to fend off the 2021 Derby winner **Adayar** (128) by half a length, with **My Prospero** (129) just a nose further back in third. The winner seemed to benefit from the return to softer ground and, granted suitable conditions, he should be capable of winning more races at the top level in 2023. Similar comments apply to stable companion **Desert Crown** (128p), who looked potentially one of the best Derby winners this century when making it three from three at Epsom, quickening clear to win by two and a half lengths in impressive fashion. He missed the rest of the season due to injury but should have more to offer as a four-year-old if making a full recovery.

Westover (126) finished a good third at Epsom and would have been second with a clear run, doing his best work late on having been badly hampered entering the

Baaeed (right) is only fourth behind Bay Bridge (left) in the Champion Stakes

final two furlongs. He confirmed the promise of that effort when subsequently running away with the Irish Derby at the Curragh, showing high-class form to land the spoils by seven lengths, though neither he nor Desert Crown was the pick of the Derby winners last year on Timeform ratings. That honour belonged to the Prix du Jockey Club hero **Vadeni** (130), who was the highest-rated three-year-old full stop having also won the Eclipse at Sandown before later hitting the frame in the Irish Champion Stakes at Leopardstown (beaten a length and three-quarters into third behind **Luxembourg** (128)) and Prix de l'Arc de Triomphe at Longchamp (beaten half a length into second behind **Alpinista** (127)).

It was a case of what might have been last year for Luxembourg, who was the ante-post favourite for the Derby after finishing a staying-on third in the 2000 Guineas but was then ruled out of Epsom due to injury. He showed what he is capable of when winning the Irish Champion, though, battling well to beat the Grand Prix de Paris winner **Onesto** (127) by half a length, and it's probably worth putting a line through his below-par run when seventh in the Arc as he reportedly pulled a muscle. By contrast, everything went smoothly for Alpinista at Longchamp as she ended her career with her eighth win in a row and her sixth at the top level, hitting the front inside the final two furlongs and always holding on from there to lead home Vadeni, the 2021 winner **Torquator Tasso** (128) and the lightly-raced three-year-old **Al Hakeem** (125).

Pyledriver (126) proved better than ever when beating Torquator Tasso by two and three-quarter lengths in the King George VI and Queen Elizabeth Stakes at

Ascot, paying a handsome compliment to **Hukum** (127), the horse he'd been over four lengths behind when runner-up in the Coronation Cup. Unfortunately, Hukum suffered a season-ending injury when winning at Epsom, but trainer Owen Burrows still had a couple of high-class middle-distance performers heading into the autumn, namely the Strensall Stakes/Darley Stakes winner **Alflaila** (125) and the Rose of Lancaster Stakes/Prix Dollar winner **Anmaat** (125). William Haggas was another trainer who had a strong hand in this division with the likes of Baaeed, My Prospero and **Alenquer** (124), who made the breakthrough in Group 1 company in the Tattersalls Gold Cup at the Curragh. Back in third on that occasion was **State of Rest** (127), who'd already won the Prix Ganay at Longchamp and resumed winning ways after in the Prince of Wales's Stakes at Royal Ascot, digging deep to beat none other than Bay Bridge on the last occasion.

Charlie Appleby continued his remarkable run in North America when **Rebel's Romance** (126)—the stable's apparent second string with William Buick choosing to ride **Nations Pride** (124)—won the Breeders' Cup Turf at Keeneland, beating **Stone Age** (122) by two and a quarter lengths to give his trainer a third success at that fixture. That tally was matched by Aidan O'Brien, who completed his hat-trick when **Tuesday** (122) won the Breeders' Cup Filly and Mare Turf, her first win since edging out **Emily Upjohn** (120) in the Oaks at Epsom. Emily Upjohn opened her own account at the top level when winning the Fillies' & Mares' Stakes at Ascot, while **Nashwa** (119) was another talented three-year-old filly for the John and Thady Gosden yard, notably winning the Prix de Diane at Chantilly and Nassau Stakes at Goodwood before running with credit in the Prix de l'Opera at Longchamp (beaten three quarters of a length into second behind **Place du Carrousel** (120)) and Breeders' Cup Filly and Mare Turf (beaten three and a half lengths into fourth behind Tuesday).

Stayers

It was the end of an era in this division as the retirement of **Stradivarius** (124)—Timeform's highest-rated stayer in training for three years in a row between 2018 and 2020—was announced just a few weeks after he'd been forced to miss the Lonsdale Cup at York due to a bruised foot. Stradivarius wasn't the invincible force of old in 2021 and it was a similar story last season, but he still showed himself to be capable of very smart form in three starts, winning the Yorkshire Cup at York before hitting the frame in his attempts to win a fourth Gold Cup and a fifth Goodwood Cup. Tremendously tough and reliable, Stradivarius won a record 18 pattern races in his glittering career and will be remembered as one of the best stayers in the modern era.

Kyprios (131) quickly cemented his own place in that illustrious company as he went unbeaten in six starts last season, proving himself a top-class performer and achieving a higher Timeform rating than Stradivarius ever did in his career. Kyprios

Kyprios wins a memorable edition of the Goodwood Cup

gained his first Group 1 success when beating **Mojo Star** (123) by half a length in the Gold Cup at Royal Ascot, with another three quarters of a length back to Stradivarius, who endured a troubled passage on his way to finishing third. However, any doubts about the winner's superiority were quickly dispelled as he continued to sweep all before him with further wins in the Goodwood Cup, Irish St Leger at the Curragh and Prix du Cadran at Longchamp. He saved his best performance for last in France where he won by a record-equalling margin for a Group 1, ultimately landing the spoils by 20 lengths. He did that despite almost running sideways for much of the final furlong, an extraordinary display and, in pure form terms, one of the best by a stayer for years.

If that was a one-horse race, then the Goodwood Cup was memorable for bringing together several gifted stayers. Kyprios typically showed a willing attitude to hold off Stradivarius by a neck, while the pair who followed them home, **Trueshan** (128) and **Coltrane** (120), both enjoyed very productive campaigns of their own. Forced to miss the Gold Cup due to quicker-than-ideal ground, Trueshan instead waited for the Northumberland Plate at Newcastle where, from a BHA mark of 120, he put up a remarkable weight-carrying performance to win by half a length from a horse to whom he was conceding 23 lb. Admittedly, Trueshan failed to match that effort in three subsequent runs, but he still managed to hit the frame in both the Goodwood Cup and Doncaster Cup before regaining the winning thread in the Long Distance Cup. He was beaten a neck by Coltrane on Town Moor, but the tables were turned after another titanic tussle between the pair at Ascot, with Trueshan ultimately getting the verdict by a head to win that race for the third year in a row.

Quickthorn (119) benefited from an enterprising ride to win the Lonsdale Cup by 14 lengths from Coltrane, his third pattern-race victory in a row having previously struck in the Henry II Stakes at Sandown and Prix Maurice de Nieuil at Longchamp. He struggled for form after his York success, however, finishing down the field in the Prix du Cadran and Long Distance Cup. The other major disappointments in the Long Distance Cup were **Eldar Eldarov** (121) and **Waterville** (117), both three-year-olds who arrived at Ascot on an upward curve. Eldar Eldarov had put up a career-best effort to win the St Leger at Doncaster, staying on strongly to land the spoils by two lengths in the style of one likely to be suited by going up in trip. The unexposed filly **Haskoy** (116p) was second past the post but badly hampered **Giavelletto** (113) and was subsequently demoted two places by the stewards. As for Waterville, he was a tailed-off last at Ascot but is perhaps better judged on the form he showed when coming from what looked a most unpromising position turning in to win the Irish Cesarewitch at the Curragh.

New London (120), the beaten favourite in the St Leger (when promoted to second), had previously won the Gordon Stakes at Goodwood, asserting late on to win by a length and three-quarters from **Deauville Legend** (121), with another neck back to the Derby runner-up **Ho Ya Mal** (119) in third. Deauville Legend went on to win the Great Voltigeur Stakes at York and fared best of the European contingent when fourth in the Melbourne Cup at Flemington. Closer to home, **Hamish** (124) won twice in Group 3 company and threatened to give Kyprios a race in between when filling the runner-up spot in the Irish St Leger, ultimately passing the post three quarters of a length behind that rival. The Prix Royal-Oak at Longchamp was the one Group 1 race open to Kyprios in this division that he skipped and **Iresine** (123) ran out a dominant three-length winner in his absence, taking his tally to 11 wins from 15 starts.

2022 STATISTICS (In Britain)

TRAINERS (1,2,3 earnings)	Horses	Indiv'l Wnrs	Races Won	Runs	% Strike Rate	Stakes £
1 Charlie Appleby	164	98	152	488	31.1	6,013,787
2 William Haggas	183	101	167	671	24.9	5,420,107
3 John & Thady Gosden	196	95	129	591	21.8	4,912,139
4 Andrew Balding	249	96	133	927	14.3	4,161,954
5 Roger Varian	180	102	140	639	21.9	3,332,147
6 Sir Michael Stoute	85	29	36	247	14.6	2,809,123
7 K. R. Burke	164	77	117	783	14.9	2,702,344
8 Charlie & Mark Johnston	214	105	176	1,267	13.9	2,694,810
9 Ralph Beckett	161	62	88	565	15.6	2,487,770
10 Aidan O'Brien, Ireland	51	13	15	84	17.9	2,428,482

JOCKEYS (by winners)	1st	2nd	3rd	Unpl	Total Rides	% Strike Rate
1 William Buick	201	127	105	317	750	26.8
2 Hollie Doyle	151	142	135	577	1005	15.0
3 David Probert	144	141	134	727	1146	12.6
4 Daniel Muscutt	128	123	110	491	852	15.0
5 Tom Marquand	127	93	118	551	889	14.3
6 Kevin Stott	116	96	107	439	758	15.3
7 Rossa Ryan	116	110	81	463	770	15.1
8 Jack Mitchell	112	88	82	350	632	17.7
9 Daniel Tudhope	111	87	76	399	673	16.5
10 Paul Mulrennan	108	91	85	431	715	15.1

SIRES OF WINNERS (1,2,3 earnings)	Races Won	Runs	% Strike Rate	Stakes £
1 Dubawi (by Dubai Millennium)	142	605	23.5	5,781,970
2 Sea The Stars (by Cape Cross)	86	490	17.6	4,550,525
3 Frankel (by Galileo)	97	554	17.5	3,687,972
4 Dark Angel (by Acclamation)	170	1294	13.1	2,938,293
5 New Bay (by Dubawi)	62	322	19.3	2,871,621
6 Kingman (by Invincible Spirit)	96	630	15.2	2,855,313
7 Galileo (by Sadler's Wells)	37	261	14.2	2,143,076
8 Lope de Vega (by Shamardal)	128	842	15.2	2,128,278
9 Kodiac (by Danehill)	170	1559	10.9	2,077,347
10 Nathaniel (by Galileo)	55	415	13.3	1,997,574

LEADING HORSES (1,2,3 earnings)	Races Won	% Strike Rate	Stakes £
1 Baaeed 4 b.c Sea The Stars - Aghareed	4	80.0	1,672,945
2 Bay Bridge 4 b.c New Bay - Hayyona	2	50.0	1,011,040
3 Desert Crown 3 b.c Nathaniel - Desert Berry	2	100.0	1,008,870
4 Pyledriver 5 b.h Harbour Watch - La Pyle	1	50.0	804,550
5 Naval Crown 4 b.c Dubawi - Come Alive	1	25.0	702,228
6 Bayside Boy 3 b.c New Bay - Alava	2	50.0	685,900
7 Kinross 5 b.g Kingman - Ceilidh House	3	50.0	625,750
8 State Of Rest 4 b.c Starspangledbanner - Repose	1	100.0	613,984
9 Eldar Eldarov 3 b.c Dubawi - All At Sea	3	75.0	605,083
10 Kyprios 4 ch.c Galileo - Polished Gem	2	100.0	567,100

SECTION

5

THE TIMEFORM TOP 100

2 Year Olds

126p	Little Big Bear
121p	Auguste Rodin
119p	Noble Style
118	Blackbeard
118	Chaldean
118	Royal Scotsman
116P	Tahiyra
115p	Sakheer
115	Silver Knott
114p	Al Riffa
114p	Victoria Road
114	Blue Rose Cen
114	Marshman
114	Meditate
113	Bradsell
113	Mischief Magic
112p	Commissioning
112p	Nostrum
112	Dubai Mile
112	Lezoo
111p	Arrest
111	Al Dasim
111	Belbek
111	Eddie's Boy
111	Epictetus
111	Mysterious Night
111	The Antarctic
111	The Platinum Queen
111	Trillium
110p	Espionage
110	Aesop's Fables
110	Gamestop
110	Love Reigns
110	Proud And Regal
109	Breizh Sky
109	Cold Case
109	Crypto Force
109	Naval Power
108p	Dream of Love
108p	Knight
108	Beauty Crescent
108	Holloway Boy
108	Novakai
108	Persian Force
108	Shartash
107p	Alpenjager
107p	Charyn
107p	The Foxes
107	Indestructible
107	Marbaan
107	Mawj
106p	Flying Honours
106p	Salt Bay
106	Dramatised
106	Rumstar
105p	Continuous
105p	Statuette
105	Never Just A Dream
105	Prince of Pillo
105	Shouldvebeenaring
104p	Blanchland
104p	Electric Eyes
104p	Streets of Gold
104	Alpha Capture
104	Kyeema
104	Swingalong
103p	Local Dynasty
103p	Midnight Mile
103p	Tarjeeh
103p	Victory Dance
103	Brave Emperor
103	Dancing Magic
103	Grey's Monument
103	Isaac Shelby
103	Queen Me
103	Rocket Rodney
103	The Ridler
102p	Amichi
102p	Desert Order
102p	Lose Yourself
102	Al Karrar
102	Bresson
102	Galeron
102	Legend of Xanadu
102	Matilda Picotte
102	Proverb
102	Show Respect
102	Walbank
101	Greenland
101	Heavenly Breath
101	Juliet Sierra
101	Lady Hollywood
101	Looking For Lynda
101	Magical Sunset
101	One Nation
100p	Fantastic Moon
100	Age of Kings
100	Chateau
100	Crispy Cat
100	Highbank
100	Maylandsea
100	Olivia Maralda
100	Rage of Bamby
100	Rousing Encore
100	Treasure Trove
100	Tyrone's Poppy
100	Wahaaj
100	Wodao

3 Year Olds

130	Equinox
130	Nest
130	Vadeni
129	My Prospero
128p	Desert Crown
128	Jack Christopher
128	Luxembourg
127p	Charge It
127	Coroebus
127	Onesto
127	Serifos
126	Boldog Hos
126	Taiba
126	Westover
125	Al Hakeem
125	Alflaila
125	Native Trail
124	El Bodegon
124	Inspiral
124	Mo Donegal
124	Nations Pride
123	Bayside Boy
123	Homeless Songs
122	Erevann
122	Junko
122	Light Infantry
122	Manaccan
122	Modern Games
122	Stone Age
122	Tuesday
122	Tunnes
121p	Maljoom
121	Deauville Legend
121	Do Deuce
121	Early Voting
121	Eldar Eldarov
121	Missed The Cut
121	Rich Strike
121	Sense of Duty
120	Emily Upjohn
120	New London
120	Place du Carrousel
120	Sammarco
119	Fonteyn
119	Hoo Ya Mal
119	Nashwa
119	Ottoman Fleet
119	Perfect Power
119	Simca Mille
118	Annaf
118	Cresta
118	Crown Pride
118	Lassaut
118	Mitbaahy
118	Schwarzer Peter
118	So Moonstruck
118	Spendarella
117p	Francesco Clemente
117p	Laurel
117p	Manaafith
117	Checkandchallenge
117	Eternal Pearl
117	I'm A Gambler
117	La Parisienne
117	Mighty Ulysses
117	Tenebrism
117	Warren Point

117	Waterville	130	Knicks Go	123	Kinross	119	Quickthorn
117	Zagrey	129	Bay Bridge	123	Mojo Star	119	Royal Champion
116p	Eydon	129	Golden Pal	123	Panthalassa	119	Sir Busker
116p	Haskoy	129	Romantic Warrior	122p	Free Wind	119	Siskany
116	Above The Curve	129	Titleholder	122	Botanik	119	Storm Damage
116	Angel Bleu	128	Adayar	122	Mostahdaf	119	Tashkhan
116	Dhabab	128	Golden Sixty	122	Pretty Tiger	119	The Revenant
116	El Caballo	128	Home Affairs	122	Sealiway		
116	Go Bears Go	128	Torquator Tasso	122	Sonnyboyliston		
116	Israr	128	Trueshan	122	Stay Foolish		
116	Lusail	127	Alpinista	122§	Al Aasy		
116	New Energy	127	Hukum	121	Baratti		
116	Noble Truth	127	Minzaal	121	Bathrat Leon		
116	Phantom Flight	127	Mishriff	121	Bubble Gift		
116	Prosperous Voyage	127	State of Rest	121	Egot		
116	Stay Alert	126	Anamoe	121	Grocer Jack		
116	With The Moonlight	126	California Spangle	121	Mendocino		
115+	Zechariah	126	Country Grammer	121	Pearls Galore		
115	Blue Trail	126	Eduardo	121	Rohaan		
115	Boundless Ocean	126	Highfield Princess	121	Saffron Beach		
115	Changingoftheguard	126	Hurricane Lane	121	Skalleti		
115	Flaming Rib	126	Malathaat	121	Valiant Prince		
115	Harry Three	126	Pyledriver	121	Win Marilyn		
115	Royal Aclaim	126	Rebel's Romance	121?	Naval Crown		
115	Secret State	126	Vela Azul	120	Addeybb		
115	Triple Time	126	Wellington	120	Coltrane		
115	West Wind Blows	125	Anmaat	120	Creative Force		
115	Wild Crusade	125	Emblem Road	120	Escobar		
114	Audience	125	Gold Trip	120	Grand Glory		
114	Bolthole	125	Goodnight Olive	120	Lord Glitters		
114	Caturra	125	Hot Rod Charlie	120	Switzerland		
114	Duke de Sessa	125	Lord North	120	Waikuku		
114	Fast Response	125	Olympiad	119	Al Suhail		
114	Inverness	125	Real World	119	Artorius		
114	Ladies Church	125	Salios	119	Baron Samedi		
114	Malavath	125	Scope	119	Commanche Falls		
114	Mimikyu	125	Shahryar	119	Deep Bond		
114	Point Lonsdale	125	Yibir	119	Dubai Honour		
114	Tacarib Bay	124	Aldaary	119	Fancy Man		
14	The Grey Wizard	124	Alenquer	119	Grenadier Guards		
		124	Cody's Wish	119	Ilaraab		
		124	Elite Power	119	Jadoomi		
Older Horses		124	Hamish	119	Lazuli		
143	Flightline	124	Master of The Seas	119	Manobo		
137	Baaeed	124	Stradivarius	119	Mare Australis		
132	Jackie's Warrior	123	Alcohol Free	119	Megallan		
131	Kyprios	123	Algiers	119	Mujtaba		
131	Life Is Good	123	Dreamloper	119	Mutasaabeq		
131	Nature Strip	123	Iresine	119	Nahaarr		

TRAINERS FOR COURSES

The following statistics show the most successful trainers over the past five seasons at each of the courses that stage Flat racing in England, Scotland and Wales. Impact Value is expressed as a factor of a trainer's number of winners compared to those expected to occur by chance. Market Value is expressed as the factor by which the % chance of an Industry Starting Price exceeds random, as implied by field size. For example, a horse that is shorter than 3/1 in a 4-runner field will have a market value above 1.

ASCOT

Trainer	Wins	Runs	Strike Rate	% Rivals Beaten	P/L	Run To Form %	Impact Value	Market Value
John Gosden	34	173	19.65%	58.56	-26.48	48.86	2.06	2.11
William Haggas	31	207	14.98%	57.75	-74.57	40.50	1.56	1.88
Andrew Balding	30	289	10.38%	52.44	-64.31	44.46	1.09	1.20
Charlie Appleby	28	165	16.97%	57.34	-30.74	44.21	1.78	2.05
Roger Varian	25	194	12.89%	55.53	-17.55	40.74	1.48	1.53
Aidan O'Brien, Ireland	23	254	9.06%	51.57	-135.61	45.85	0.99	1.69
Clive Cox	20	155	12.90%	54.77	135.10	45.16	1.50	1.35
John & Thady Gosden	16	112	14.29%	56.34	6.88	54.46	1.50	1.98
Mark Johnston	16	197	8.12%	48.85	-98.63	38.07	0.91	1.18
Ed Walker	16	104	15.38%	54.74	-1.67	44.23	1.75	1.48

AYR

Trainer	Wins	Runs	Strike Rate	% Rivals Beaten	P/L	Run To Form %	Impact Value	Market Value
Jim Goldie	54	548	9.85%	48.27	-121.38	33.64	0.89	1.01
Keith Dalgleish	42	501	8.38%	49.24	-207.53	34.28	0.76	1.05
Richard Fahey	35	336	10.42%	52.97	-107.20	38.15	1.01	1.24
Tim Easterby	32	262	12.21%	55.44	40.68	38.97	1.29	1.44
David O'Meara	32	225	14.22%	56.45	-6.34	41.58	1.26	1.46
R. Mike Smith	30	261	11.49%	45.87	21.38	31.09	1.05	0.88
Iain Jardine	29	279	10.39%	48.27	-47.63	31.99	0.94	0.99
Michael Dods	24	253	9.49%	52.45	-108.42	35.89	0.90	1.42
Mark Johnston	23	151	15.23%	52.41	-58.59	37.03	1.13	1.42
Kevin Ryan	22	197	11.17%	49.26	-80.78	32.82	1.13	1.34

BATH

Trainer	Wins	Runs	Strike Rate	% Rivals Beaten	P/L	Run To Form %	Impact Value	Market Value
Tony Carroll	30	246	12.20%	50.24	-62.95	28.57	1.09	1.05
Clive Cox	28	107	26.17%	64.75	35.64	50.07	2.09	1.80
Mark Johnston	26	92	28.26%	63.69	12.90	53.87	1.77	1.63
Rod Millman	21	144	14.58%	51.23	23.71	39.93	1.22	1.11
Ronald Harris	18	160	11.25%	51.33	-30.71	32.79	0.96	1.09
Adrian Wintle	17	78	21.79%	62.25	44.83	47.44	2.07	1.43
Mick Channon	16	94	17.02%	55.24	-13.88	38.10	1.50	1.38
Eve Johnson Houghton	15	99	15.15%	58.13	-11.63	41.66	1.23	1.45
Richard Hannon	15	135	11.11%	51.63	-69.52	33.68	0.87	1.38
David Evans	13	102	12.75%	49.57	-18.98	28.97	1.09	1.16

BEVERLEY

Trainer	Wins	Runs	Strike Rate	% Rivals Beaten	P/L	Run To Form %	Impact Value	Market Value
Tim Easterby	52	481	10.81%	50.03	-156.43	33.29	1.01	1.15
Mark Johnston	40	172	23.26%	57.29	-35.89	47.04	1.74	1.80
David O'Meara	38	226	16.81%	57.55	26.31	41.19	1.47	1.42
Richard Fahey	38	316	12.03%	52.10	-97.99	38.71	1.08	1.31
Nigel Tinkler	29	222	13.06%	50.67	48.95	36.47	1.28	1.05
Kevin Ryan	21	137	15.33%	58.42	-46.02	43.19	1.39	1.61
Paul Midgley	18	163	11.04%	54.92	-55.84	34.97	1.08	1.17
Roger Fell	15	160	9.38%	45.11	-14.33	23.26	0.89	1.08
Michael & David Easterby	14	72	19.44%	58.30	19.19	44.79	1.84	1.15
Bryan Smart	11	105	10.48%	55.33	-39.08	40.47	0.99	1.19

BRIGHTON

Trainer	Wins	Runs	Strike Rate	% Rivals Beaten	P/L	Run To Form %	Impact Value	Market Value
Tony Carroll	53	404	13.12%	50.92	-119.06	34.83	0.99	1.18
Richard Hannon	25	117	21.37%	60.88	22.87	46.70	1.46	1.43
Gary Moore	23	169	13.61%	50.99	-33.98	33.27	1.13	1.39
Eve Johnson Houghton	19	107	17.76%	54.29	10.06	37.71	1.30	1.38
John Gallagher	16	104	15.38%	48.25	6.70	33.14	1.14	1.11
Stuart Williams	14	68	20.59%	55.83	18.25	41.18	1.48	1.41
Andrew Balding	14	56	25.00%	58.49	3.28	48.21	1.54	1.48
Michael Attwater	13	108	12.04%	50.48	-48.22	38.59	0.84	0.93
Archie Watson	13	59	22.03%	56.09	-0.08	37.92	1.36	1.48
George Baker	12	88	13.64%	57.74	-33.18	42.05	0.99	1.50

CARLISLE

Trainer	Wins	Runs	Strike Rate	% Rivals Beaten	P/L	Run To Form %	Impact Value	Market Value
Tim Easterby	24	304	7.89%	50.01	-65.92	32.35	0.72	1.17
Keith Dalgleish	23	183	12.57%	51.28	-16.50	31.11	1.08	1.15
Richard Fahey	22	171	12.87%	53.19	-17.13	33.67	1.19	1.21
K. R. Burke	18	99	18.18%	59.73	-5.45	49.37	1.54	1.60
Mark Johnston	16	69	23.19%	65.06	29.46	54.98	1.75	1.45
Dianne Sayer	15	79	18.99%	53.68	10.20	45.95	1.64	1.42
Kevin Ryan	14	87	16.09%	58.18	-37.66	46.38	1.38	1.54
Nigel Tinkler	11	48	22.92%	55.53	39.41	37.50	2.14	1.31
Roger Fell	11	82	13.41%	55.97	-11.38	37.24	1.25	1.20
Michael Dods	9	122	7.38%	51.94	-80.30	35.74	0.69	1.30

CATTERICK BRIDGE

Trainer	Wins	Runs	Strike Rate	% Rivals Beaten	P/L	Run To Form %	Impact Value	Market Value
Tim Easterby	40	388	10.31%	53.49	-91.18	32.17	0.95	1.13
David O'Meara	24	168	14.29%	51.46	-84.94	28.82	1.24	1.55
Richard Fahey	23	180	12.78%	56.39	-41.37	35.10	1.13	1.25
Keith Dalgleish	21	122	17.21%	55.84	67.71	38.59	1.48	1.29
K. R. Burke	16	84	19.05%	54.42	10.73	42.80	1.59	1.44
Mark Johnston	15	101	14.85%	53.40	-32.89	44.09	1.11	1.46
Michael Dods	15	96	15.63%	55.00	36.50	40.38	1.49	1.53
John Quinn	14	149	9.40%	50.82	-74.38	28.90	0.86	1.32
Brian Ellison	13	75	17.33%	57.92	8.52	40.28	1.53	1.36
Paul Midgley	12	73	16.44%	51.76	-5.78	33.34	1.43	1.35

CHELMSFORD CITY (AW)

Trainer	Wins	Runs	Strike Rate	% Rivals Beaten	P/L	Run To Form %	Impact Value	Market Value
Michael Appleby	76	632	12.03%	52.02	-132.38	35.14	1.04	1.20
Mark Johnston	71	411	17.27%	55.29	-27.42	48.01	1.27	1.34
Stuart Williams	55	425	12.94%	55.52	-156.41	39.40	1.11	1.40
John Gosden	51	186	27.42%	69.39	-24.95	60.77	2.13	2.32
Richard Hughes	50	238	21.01%	61.55	78.33	54.34	1.82	1.49
David Simcock	50	301	16.61%	54.35	-44.67	39.87	1.21	1.16
Saeed bin Suroor	40	176	22.73%	62.30	-34.29	53.48	1.84	2.08
Henry Spiller	34	253	13.44%	50.06	53.83	30.31	1.30	1.16
Archie Watson	32	228	14.04%	55.85	-33.41	45.09	1.11	1.48
Dean Ivory	30	305	9.84%	50.68	-91.15	29.93	0.93	1.12

CHEPSTOW

Trainer	Wins	Runs	Strike Rate	% Rivals Beaten	P/L	Run To Form %	Impact Value	Market Value
David Evans	22	172	12.79%	49.27	-26.52	33.43	1.10	1.12
Tony Carroll	20	164	12.20%	52.11	0.70	40.94	1.13	1.12
John O'Shea	20	146	13.70%	43.67	-5.93	24.81	1.16	1.01
Ralph Beckett	18	56	32.14%	64.92	18.64	56.28	2.40	1.86
Rod Millman	15	122	12.30%	56.50	-41.13	36.89	1.02	1.31
Mick Channon	14	97	14.43%	52.67	5.45	39.63	1.24	1.42
Eve Johnson Houghton	13	72	18.06%	57.33	-4.06	37.57	1.43	1.60
Christopher Mason	11	95	11.58%	50.88	-7.29	26.89	1.02	0.98
Richard Hannon	10	110	9.09%	51.25	-40.50	34.72	0.76	1.46
Grace Harris	10	123	8.13%	40.27	7.83	19.27	0.73	0.77

CHESTER

Trainer	Wins	Runs	Strike Rate	% Rivals Beaten	P/L	Run To Form %	Impact Value	Market Value
Richard Fahey	40	378	10.58%	52.88	-80.34	32.80	0.92	1.27
Andrew Balding	40	194	20.62%	60.66	-10.64	57.73	1.57	1.72
Tom Dascombe	36	245	14.69%	52.37	-60.38	41.85	1.15	1.20
Mark Johnston	22	151	14.57%	55.35	-25.57	49.34	1.13	1.47
Tim Easterby	21	172	12.21%	50.73	-22.63	36.63	1.08	1.18
Ralph Beckett	18	76	23.68%	58.64	-15.18	51.32	1.83	1.66
Ian Williams	17	199	8.54%	47.63	-83.50	35.18	0.77	1.11
Aidan O'Brien, Ireland	12	28	42.86%	71.28	20.89	75.00	3.01	1.62
William Haggas	11	43	25.58%	62.72	-6.03	55.81	1.77	2.14
David Evans	10	66	15.15%	50.16	-3.50	36.36	1.33	1.11

DONCASTER

Trainer	Wins	Runs	Strike Rate	% Rivals Beaten	P/L	Run To Form %	Impact Value	Market Value
Richard Hannon	35	281	12.46%	54.41	-35.93	45.31	1.09	1.29
Roger Varian	35	156	22.44%	66.14	-41.18	54.05	1.88	2.31
Richard Fahey	27	294	9.18%	51.06	-62.55	33.74	0.90	1.08
William Haggas	24	122	19.67%	65.46	12.81	51.93	1.81	2.12
Andrew Balding	24	110	21.82%	61.62	82.25	55.25	1.98	1.57
Charlie Appleby	19	76	25.00%	62.38	-13.28	49.26	1.91	2.83
Ralph Beckett	19	105	18.10%	59.41	18.37	54.97	1.63	1.73
John & Thady Gosden	18	70	25.71%	63.85	12.67	51.76	2.14	2.09
Sir Michael Stoute	18	76	23.68%	65.32	-15.09	56.58	1.77	2.19
David O'Meara	17	221	7.69%	51.40	-103.25	31.94	0.75	1.11

EPSOM

Trainer	Wins	Runs	Strike Rate	% Rivals Beaten	P/L	Run To Form %	Impact Value	Market Value
Jim Boyle	19	123	15.45%	51.27	-2.08	44.44	1.22	1.06
Andrew Balding	15	96	15.63%	58.07	-35.35	47.42	1.28	1.62
Charlie Appleby	11	34	32.35%	65.27	35.29	58.82	2.39	1.71
Ralph Beckett	10	52	19.23%	56.28	-11.92	50.00	1.47	1.40
Mick Channon	9	48	18.75%	58.26	-0.97	35.42	1.46	1.30
Mark Johnston	9	78	11.54%	51.72	-26.09	42.31	0.86	1.31
Gary Moore	8	55	14.55%	47.86	24.95	27.64	1.09	1.01
David O'Meara	7	60	11.67%	52.32	-13.50	35.00	1.02	1.12
Simon Dow	7	52	13.46%	45.76	0.25	36.00	1.11	0.88
Aidan O'Brien, Ireland	7	55	12.73%	55.49	7.60	52.73	1.34	1.37

FFOS LAS

Trainer	Wins	Runs	Strike Rate	% Rivals Beaten	P/L	Run To Form %	Impact Value	Market Value
Rod Millman	13	73	17.81%	52.98	-3.79	34.81	1.40	1.14
Andrew Balding	13	59	22.03%	65.04	-3.51	51.13	1.70	2.11
Archie Watson	9	37	24.32%	55.75	0.25	44.26	1.72	1.55
Hughie Morrison	9	32	28.13%	61.78	26.56	43.75	2.38	1.63
Ed Walker	7	38	18.42%	65.84	9.10	52.35	1.35	1.15
Richard Hughes	7	40	17.50%	58.69	6.62	47.50	1.48	1.62
David Evans	7	105	6.67%	40.27	-58.00	28.25	0.53	0.84
Ralph Beckett	7	31	22.58%	59.33	10.75	54.84	1.79	1.88
Roger Charlton	6	30	20.00%	62.04	28.44	41.67	1.63	1.88
Jamie Osborne	6	24	25.00%	70.44	26.50	69.61	1.90	1.35

GOODWOOD

Trainer	Wins	Runs	Strike Rate	% Rivals Beaten	P/L	Run To Form %	Impact Value	Market Value
Andrew Balding	38	243	15.64%	56.95	-52.68	53.31	1.32	1.37
Mark Johnston	36	264	13.64%	52.18	-87.66	40.39	1.24	1.34
William Haggas	29	140	20.71%	61.64	-11.22	55.39	1.75	1.94
Richard Hannon	20	286	6.99%	47.24	-115.25	36.66	0.65	1.04
Charlie Appleby	19	69	27.54%	65.68	-6.53	54.46	2.26	2.17
Ralph Beckett	19	123	15.45%	52.73	9.52	47.15	1.35	1.43
Charles Hills	17	134	12.69%	51.94	-30.15	36.81	1.13	1.30
Clive Cox	15	94	15.96%	51.78	-9.25	43.04	1.37	1.27
David Menuisier	14	65	21.54%	45.67	32.80	39.01	1.89	1.05
John Gosden	13	64	20.31%	60.71	-22.75	55.84	1.59	1.92

HAMILTON

Trainer	Wins	Runs	Strike Rate	% Rivals Beaten	P/L	Run To Form %	Impact Value	Market Value
Keith Dalgleish	49	399	12.28%	50.34	-21.51	36.47	0.95	1.08
Richard Fahey	40	226	17.70%	55.25	-42.11	43.75	1.32	1.27
Jim Goldie	33	265	12.45%	48.70	-79.55	35.49	1.07	1.00
Tim Easterby	32	215	14.88%	57.49	-49.03	41.11	1.28	1.50
Kevin Ryan	31	140	22.14%	58.25	-11.87	50.97	1.62	1.45
Mark Johnston	30	155	19.35%	56.99	-26.34	46.45	1.38	1.59
David O'Meara	27	147	18.37%	56.76	-32.32	41.84	1.41	1.52
Iain Jardine	22	256	8.59%	48.20	-89.53	31.45	0.71	0.97
Roger Fell	12	91	13.19%	54.03	-45.54	36.26	1.20	1.40
Julie Camacho	10	28	35.71%	64.06	18.03	45.83	2.74	1.75

HAYDOCK PARK

Trainer	Wins	Runs	Strike Rate	% Rivals Beaten	P/L	Run To Form %	Impact Value	Market Value
William Haggas	43	179	24.02%	66.16	-32.22	59.97	1.84	2.04
Tom Dascombe	42	303	13.86%	52.30	55.82	39.35	1.14	1.24
Mark Johnston	31	213	14.55%	53.38	-42.77	41.00	1.06	1.21
David O'Meara	25	212	11.79%	50.19	12.15	34.34	0.95	1.10
Ed Walker	25	130	19.23%	55.73	4.31	48.38	1.57	1.43
Richard Hannon	25	182	13.74%	53.37	-41.54	42.20	1.14	1.21
Tim Easterby	23	309	7.44%	47.04	-117.45	28.63	0.70	0.95
Ralph Beckett	22	91	24.18%	59.07	6.05	54.69	1.93	1.84
Kevin Ryan	21	173	12.14%	50.78	-40.25	33.24	0.99	1.12
Charles Hills	19	86	22.09%	57.50	51.44	42.82	1.71	1.21

KEMPTON PARK (AW)

Trainer	Wins	Runs	Strike Rate	% Rivals Beaten	P/L	Run To Form %	Impact Value	Market Value
Roger Varian	72	297	24.24%	68.67	-4.24	55.07	2.40	2.43
Andrew Balding	64	441	14.51%	58.76	18.25	47.24	1.35	1.45
Richard Hannon	62	604	10.26%	51.74	-183.65	38.16	0.99	1.22
John Gosden	62	238	26.05%	68.76	-25.75	57.74	2.45	2.67
Charlie Appleby	59	171	34.50%	77.02	-29.76	71.09	3.18	3.68
Archie Watson	48	290	16.55%	54.87	-82.21	39.23	1.49	1.58
Ralph Beckett	46	283	16.25%	59.45	-42.47	45.69	1.58	1.70
Clive Cox	44	342	12.87%	55.24	-54.07	40.17	1.30	1.47
Marco Botti	43	403	10.67%	56.03	-0.47	44.87	1.05	1.25
William Haggas	42	218	19.27%	63.18	-60.44	50.51	1.79	2.24

LEICESTER

Trainer	Wins	Runs	Strike Rate	% Rivals Beaten	P/L	Run To Form %	Impact Value	Market Value
Michael Appleby	19	134	14.18%	49.60	140.28	35.82	1.19	0.99
Richard Hannon	18	156	11.54%	49.40	-54.37	35.59	0.92	1.19
Sir Michael Stoute	17	57	29.82%	68.93	3.84	64.43	2.08	1.75
Clive Cox	17	116	14.66%	53.40	1.11	44.77	1.24	1.34
Richard Fahey	17	128	13.28%	54.69	-32.22	41.67	1.16	1.33
Roger Varian	16	63	25.40%	66.16	-4.99	57.74	2.00	2.10
Saeed bin Suroor	15	53	28.30%	70.69	-2.01	65.09	2.18	2.45
Ralph Beckett	15	68	22.06%	57.67	-2.94	47.67	1.52	1.84
David Evans	14	95	14.74%	53.92	-35.01	32.83	1.24	1.24
Mark Johnston	14	92	15.22%	50.21	-25.71	41.68	1.01	1.24

LINGFIELD PARK (AW)

Trainer	Wins	Runs	Strike Rate	% Rivals Beaten	P/L	Run To Form %	Impact Value	Market Value
Archie Watson	68	342	19.88%	57.59	-23.84	44.02	1.63	1.57
Mark Johnston	57	300	19.00%	53.79	-10.14	50.17	1.43	1.41
Richard Hannon	57	429	13.29%	53.26	-100.01	43.25	1.11	1.31
John Gosden	47	161	29.19%	74.50	3.28	68.82	2.33	2.61
Gary Moore	41	344	11.92%	50.36	-69.33	32.55	1.16	1.20
Andrew Balding	39	225	17.33%	54.92	4.68	47.67	1.36	1.49
Richard Hughes	38	262	14.50%	57.23	-60.60	46.51	1.19	1.36
Tony Carroll	37	376	9.84%	48.63	-84.63	31.43	0.88	1.06
William Haggas	36	153	23.53%	68.07	-32.17	58.01	1.94	2.31
David Evans	35	291	12.03%	50.39	-64.49	32.74	1.03	1.13

LINGFIELD PARK (TURF)

Trainer	Wins	Runs	Strike Rate	% Rivals Beaten	P/L	Run To Form %	Impact Value	Market Value
Richard Hannon	17	100	17.00%	58.37	-23.56	38.58	1.41	1.67
William Haggas	12	39	30.77%	64.75	-4.18	55.31	2.21	2.10
Mick Channon	12	76	15.79%	59.83	-29.79	49.68	1.27	1.37
Archie Watson	10	49	20.41%	61.45	21.60	52.69	1.44	1.53
Gary Moore	10	83	12.05%	49.85	0.21	29.31	1.01	1.13
Andrew Balding	10	46	21.74%	56.29	3.14	42.75	1.53	1.69
John Bridger	9	102	8.82%	44.01	31.71	22.96	0.80	0.76
Charles Hills	8	29	27.59%	71.95	-5.88	53.32	2.25	1.76
Rae Guest	8	25	32.00%	58.04	42.20	40.00	2.49	1.35
Jim Boyle	8	56	14.29%	51.44	11.88	32.37	1.27	1.19

MUSSELBURGH

Trainer	Wins	Runs	Strike Rate	% Rivals Beaten	P/L	Run To Form %	Impact Value	Market Value
Keith Dalgleish	55	431	12.76%	51.63	-64.08	34.93	1.03	1.14
Iain Jardine	34	249	13.65%	48.18	18.54	38.44	1.09	1.04
Richard Fahey	33	178	18.54%	55.89	8.16	43.48	1.43	1.26
Mark Johnston	27	144	18.75%	58.02	18.69	49.99	1.32	1.50
Jim Goldie	26	277	9.39%	50.49	-89.68	29.94	0.81	1.02
Tim Easterby	26	237	10.97%	50.60	-66.83	32.20	0.89	1.31
David O'Meara	16	99	16.16%	55.84	-16.42	40.40	1.22	1.58
K. R. Burke	14	83	16.87%	49.35	-19.88	35.31	1.07	1.23
Rebecca Bastiman	12	109	11.01%	59.47	-21.25	33.35	1.03	1.11
Paul Midgley	11	112	9.82%	47.72	-44.34	28.57	0.87	1.28

NEWBURY

Trainer	Wins	Runs	Strike Rate	% Rivals Beaten	P/L	Run To Form %	Impact Value	Market Value
Richard Hannon	55	473	11.63%	54.00	-39.62	41.42	1.17	1.23
William Haggas	45	192	23.44%	62.88	0.44	50.63	2.18	2.15
Andrew Balding	31	260	11.92%	57.44	68.84	43.44	1.08	1.33
Roger Charlton	24	132	18.18%	53.93	42.37	40.67	1.81	1.46
Roger Varian	23	153	15.03%	61.23	-11.98	49.46	1.52	1.85
John Gosden	22	94	23.40%	69.28	-9.39	63.93	2.22	2.77
Charlie Appleby	21	71	29.58%	67.33	2.52	54.30	2.31	2.71
Ed Walker	21	163	12.88%	59.27	-51.90	44.17	1.32	1.41
Ralph Beckett	15	154	9.74%	49.99	-37.47	37.24	0.95	1.34
Charles Hills	14	155	9.03%	47.67	-30.25	29.32	0.93	1.05

NEWCASTLE (AW)

Trainer	Wins	Runs	Strike Rate	% Rivals Beaten	P/L	Run To Form %	Impact Value	Market Value
Richard Fahey	85	716	11.87%	54.60	-76.20	38.22	1.10	1.17
Jim Goldie	50	470	10.64%	52.53	34.50	31.17	1.06	1.19
William Haggas	45	149	30.20%	72.52	-5.17	61.19	2.38	2.53
Roger Varian	44	183	24.04%	71.46	-32.49	58.35	2.14	2.69
Antony Brittain	44	470	9.36%	52.36	-103.95	32.80	0.93	1.13
K. R. Burke	44	391	11.25%	53.79	31.40	40.01	0.99	1.24
Keith Dalgleish	40	356	11.24%	49.93	-69.98	35.77	1.09	1.26
John Gosden	39	122	31.97%	75.08	-13.95	65.28	2.50	3.04
Brian Ellison	38	398	9.55%	52.63	-136.26	37.49	0.95	1.16
Ben Haslam	37	314	11.78%	50.78	-32.29	35.81	1.15	1.21

NEWMARKET (JULY)

Trainer	Wins	Runs	Strike Rate	% Rivals Beaten	P/L	Run To Form %	Impact Value	Market Value
Charlie Appleby	59	197	29.95%	70.59	-13.34	64.43	2.25	2.34
Richard Hannon	41	311	13.18%	52.09	-65.85	41.74	1.07	1.18
John Gosden	31	132	23.48%	60.08	0.99	47.69	1.82	1.88
Mark Johnston	28	166	16.87%	49.35	-7.46	44.58	1.24	1.23
Saeed bin Suroor	23	73	31.51%	63.72	29.61	59.67	2.31	1.69
William Haggas	22	142	15.49%	58.33	-51.53	41.08	1.25	1.69
Roger Varian	18	125	14.40%	55.66	-29.13	45.95	1.11	1.54
John & Thady Gosden	16	96	16.67%	60.14	-21.81	52.50	1.16	1.66
Ralph Beckett	15	108	13.89%	55.61	-9.85	46.24	1.02	1.50
Andrew Balding	13	120	10.83%	53.09	-33.05	43.65	0.86	1.24

NEWMARKET (ROWLEY)

Trainer	Wins	Runs	Strike Rate	% Rivals Beaten	P/L	Run To Form %	Impact Value	Market Value
Charlie Appleby	87	290	30.00%	69.50	37.26	62.80	2.40	2.30
Roger Varian	41	256	16.02%	58.29	-18.50	45.87	1.50	1.61
John Gosden	39	202	19.31%	62.85	-19.20	49.72	1.70	2.00
Andrew Balding	32	252	12.70%	57.60	25.13	50.32	1.12	1.31
Mark Johnston	30	223	13.45%	48.98	-28.23	38.64	1.08	1.14
William Haggas	29	243	11.93%	52.23	-43.71	37.88	1.12	1.47
Ralph Beckett	27	171	15.79%	57.79	20.06	50.14	1.49	1.54
Richard Hannon	23	355	6.48%	47.92	-77.07	37.88	0.58	0.94
Aidan O'Brien, Ireland	17	144	11.81%	54.88	-20.64	51.39	1.11	1.68
John & Thady Gosden	16	109	14.68%	52.45	-47.01	45.72	1.28	1.72

NOTTINGHAM

Trainer	Wins	Runs	Strike Rate	% Rivals Beaten	P/L	Run To Form %	Impact Value	Market Value
Michael Appleby	37	231	16.02%	47.45	63.48	30.80	1.43	1.17
William Haggas	22	75	29.33%	68.34	8.74	59.20	2.66	2.23
Richard Hannon	19	170	11.18%	51.02	-18.75	37.81	0.95	1.10
Roger Varian	19	95	20.00%	66.35	2.12	51.28	1.73	2.13
Mark Johnston	18	122	14.75%	54.41	-50.24	45.95	1.06	1.32
K. R. Burke	17	104	16.35%	54.94	-20.56	46.92	1.28	1.35
Ian Williams	16	80	20.00%	51.74	28.04	41.80	1.79	1.25
Richard Fahey	15	150	10.00%	52.72	-50.67	40.99	0.83	1.10
Sir Michael Stoute	14	68	20.59%	63.81	9.85	52.13	1.67	1.84
Tim Easterby	13	145	8.97%	55.15	-51.96	31.72	0.87	1.10

PONTEFRACT

Trainer	Wins	Runs	Strike Rate	% Rivals Beaten	P/L	Run To Form %	Impact Value	Market Value
Richard Fahey	37	270	13.70%	54.34	8.66	37.83	1.15	1.21
Tim Easterby	31	310	10.00%	51.27	-100.88	33.39	0.87	1.07
Mark Johnston	26	159	16.35%	51.12	-36.49	38.94	1.09	1.44
David O'Meara	26	159	16.35%	54.77	-17.85	38.19	1.33	1.31
Kevin Ryan	22	148	14.86%	53.91	-26.76	39.13	1.22	1.36
Paul Midgley	20	138	14.49%	49.90	18.83	28.99	1.29	1.18
K. R. Burke	18	98	18.37%	57.02	-16.04	48.37	1.50	1.48
Roger Fell	17	98	17.35%	58.00	-6.47	35.15	1.55	1.21
Sir Michael Stoute	13	41	31.71%	63.64	8.29	46.34	1.93	2.63
Michael Dods	12	91	13.19%	49.38	2.08	31.14	1.22	1.21

REDCAR

Trainer	Wins	Runs	Strike Rate	% Rivals Beaten	P/L	Run To Form %	Impact Value	Market Value
Tim Easterby	49	555	8.83%	48.70	-90.21	29.07	0.90	1.08
David O'Meara	33	261	12.64%	54.47	-6.04	36.75	1.22	1.39
Richard Fahey	29	280	10.36%	56.29	-71.04	37.10	1.08	1.37
Michael Dods	22	250	8.80%	51.69	-42.63	32.47	0.91	1.21
William Haggas	20	63	31.75%	73.41	-8.33	61.32	2.66	2.93
Nigel Tinkler	17	203	8.37%	49.71	-59.42	29.85	0.89	1.00
Declan Carroll	16	105	15.24%	52.05	35.75	27.89	1.58	1.18
K. R. Burke	15	126	11.90%	56.26	-36.33	35.95	1.22	1.48
Mark Johnston	15	105	14.29%	48.01	-40.74	36.02	1.21	1.49
Archie Watson	13	54	24.07%	64.53	-13.30	48.68	2.33	2.31

RIPON

Trainer	Wins	Runs	Strike Rate	% Rivals Beaten	P/L	Run To Form %	Impact Value	Market Value
Tim Easterby	77	546	14.10%	52.82	-85.76	35.93	1.16	1.19
David O'Meara	45	267	16.85%	57.79	36.83	41.85	1.41	1.34
Richard Fahey	36	242	14.88%	49.05	5.42	31.71	1.20	1.20
Mark Johnston	21	167	12.57%	47.62	-55.76	35.15	0.83	1.33
William Haggas	18	52	34.62%	69.67	-11.74	54.78	2.23	2.63
Nigel Tinkler	16	120	13.33%	51.16	-9.79	28.33	1.19	1.02
Paul Midgley	11	89	12.36%	54.92	15.20	37.35	1.18	1.17
Keith Dalgleish	11	67	16.42%	52.28	-18.27	34.79	1.24	1.18
K. R. Burke	11	108	10.19%	51.19	-32.95	37.39	0.78	1.17
Roger Varian	11	32	34.38%	66.13	3.80	56.25	2.44	2.32

TRAINERS FOR COURSES

SALISBURY

Trainer	Wins	Runs	Strike Rate	% Rivals Beaten	P/L	Run To Form %	Impact Value	Market Value
Richard Hannon	30	321	9.35%	50.97	-87.52	37.71	0.76	1.17
Ralph Beckett	25	146	17.12%	58.46	-10.42	45.52	1.37	1.47
Andrew Balding	24	171	14.04%	53.34	-65.94	43.73	1.04	1.43
Clive Cox	20	112	17.86%	59.65	-6.77	46.72	1.52	1.40
Roger Varian	20	76	26.32%	66.24	-1.20	58.91	2.06	2.25
Rod Millman	16	143	11.19%	49.44	-61.59	32.17	0.97	1.10
Mick Channon	14	108	12.96%	49.46	-22.63	41.23	0.99	0.94
William Haggas	13	41	31.71%	67.15	12.24	59.80	2.52	2.46
Henry Candy	11	53	20.75%	48.69	13.87	30.64	1.80	1.12
Eve Johnson Houghton	11	92	11.96%	51.89	-21.09	34.46	0.96	1.07

SANDOWN PARK

Trainer	Wins	Runs	Strike Rate	% Rivals Beaten	P/L	Run To Form %	Impact Value	Market Value
Andrew Balding	26	187	13.90%	53.91	-44.41	47.45	1.10	1.27
Charlie Appleby	25	89	28.09%	68.16	-10.73	63.90	2.13	2.35
William Haggas	21	90	23.33%	59.68	23.48	50.98	1.88	1.79
John Gosden	21	90	23.33%	63.27	-27.61	60.66	1.86	2.26
Sir Michael Stoute	20	91	21.98%	59.99	8.19	51.65	1.78	1.78
Richard Hannon	20	198	10.10%	47.02	-48.46	35.54	0.85	0.98
John & Thady Gosden	16	68	23.53%	61.68	-17.26	53.17	1.75	2.02
David Menuisier	13	60	21.67%	55.99	19.05	56.67	2.04	1.26
Clive Cox	12	108	11.11%	48.53	-59.56	36.56	0.93	1.25
Ralph Beckett	11	90	12.22%	54.20	-32.62	41.04	1.00	1.22

SOUTHWELL (AW)

Trainer	Wins	Runs	Strike Rate	% Rivals Beaten	P/L	Run To Form %	Impact Value	Market Value
Michael Appleby	93	735	12.65%	51.98	-237.41	31.64	1.04	1.34
K. R. Burke	51	275	18.55%	59.43	74.94	44.61	1.49	1.46
Scott Dixon	45	628	7.17%	48.26	-142.33	25.47	0.64	0.94
Ivan Furtado	39	309	12.62%	53.34	-38.45	32.99	1.16	1.26
Richard Fahey	39	263	14.83%	54.68	-42.36	37.55	1.19	1.22
Tony Carroll	36	283	12.72%	51.45	68.68	29.78	1.16	1.16
Tim Easterby	31	179	17.32%	53.79	95.71	34.08	1.61	1.23
Mark Johnston	31	123	25.20%	61.23	-5.40	42.94	1.86	1.69
Antony Brittain	26	218	11.93%	57.10	-25.38	28.98	1.06	1.19
Roger Fell	24	199	12.06%	47.90	21.43	28.92	1.07	1.08

THIRSK

Trainer	Wins	Runs	Strike Rate	% Rivals Beaten	P/L	Run To Form %	Impact Value	Market Value
Tim Easterby	38	470	8.09%	47.16	-139.78	26.37	0.88	1.04
David O'Meara	33	252	13.10%	57.64	24.08	35.03	1.36	1.47
Richard Fahey	32	256	12.50%	53.99	-27.14	32.13	1.33	1.35
Michael Dods	25	266	9.40%	51.99	-65.03	32.47	1.04	1.22
Kevin Ryan	23	170	13.53%	56.94	-5.13	38.10	1.42	1.51
William Haggas	20	52	38.46%	77.57	12.99	72.01	3.20	2.99
K. R. Burke	19	106	17.92%	60.79	-7.14	45.51	1.75	1.64
Paul Midgley	15	138	10.87%	48.61	-1.25	23.34	1.27	1.18
Julie Camacho	10	97	10.31%	53.95	6.00	34.08	1.10	1.09
Declan Carroll	10	98	10.20%	52.87	10.00	28.91	1.17	1.25

WETHERBY

Trainer	Wins	Runs	Strike Rate	% Rivals Beaten	P/L	Run To Form %	Impact Value	Market Value
David O'Meara	7	36	19.44%	58.02	-6.01	42.78	1.96	1.72
Richard Fahey	5	32	15.63%	49.15	16.00	28.98	1.62	1.28
William Haggas	4	11	36.36%	66.70	2.39	63.64	3.09	2.71
John Gosden	4	9	44.44%	83.65	-0.21	50.00	4.89	4.41
Tim Easterby	3	56	5.36%	55.17	-27.50	45.68	0.55	0.90
Roger Varian	3	6	50.00%	81.82	-0.83	58.33	5.22	3.13
Declan Carroll	3	19	15.79%	62.07	8.00	42.11	1.69	1.41
Roger Fell	3	19	15.79%	60.62	-2.25	36.84	1.57	1.33
Ralph Beckett	3	4	75.00%	86.36	11.28	100.00	5.80	2.22
Archie Watson	2	8	25.00%	66.79	-1.77	62.50	2.01	2.07

WINDSOR

Trainer	Wins	Runs	Strike Rate	% Rivals Beaten	P/L	Run To Form %	Impact Value	Market Value
Richard Hannon	52	309	16.83%	59.12	13.60	43.71	1.42	1.52
Andrew Balding	29	153	18.95%	61.88	-22.24	52.37	1.59	1.67
William Haggas	27	91	29.67%	68.02	-10.23	57.07	2.55	2.67
Clive Cox	25	178	14.04%	57.58	-52.83	46.22	1.33	1.66
Eve Johnson Houghton	23	146	15.75%	53.00	-23.12	42.37	1.43	1.26
Mick Channon	22	154	14.29%	56.70	-26.51	37.45	1.29	1.39
Ralph Beckett	21	126	16.67%	61.41	-0.83	53.14	1.48	1.59
Charles Hills	16	107	14.95%	52.84	5.27	41.03	1.30	1.22
Roger Varian	15	61	24.59%	66.98	-6.37	58.31	2.18	2.39
Mark Johnston	14	64	21.88%	56.02	-6.81	56.25	1.56	1.70

TRAINERS FOR COURSES

WOLVERHAMPTON (AW)

Trainer	Wins	Runs	Strike Rate	% Rivals Beaten	P/L	Run To Form %	Impact Value	Market Value
Tony Carroll	71	712	9.97%	50.29	-65.08	34.13	0.97	1.14
David Evans	70	636	11.01%	49.11	-113.88	32.73	1.02	1.11
Michael Appleby	68	646	10.53%	49.44	-89.82	31.94	0.96	1.15
David Loughnane	64	545	11.74%	52.11	-36.86	38.80	1.09	1.17
Antony Brittain	55	532	10.34%	55.03	-101.87	36.60	0.99	1.12
Mark Loughnane	54	592	9.12%	51.59	-128.59	35.71	0.86	1.07
Mark Johnston	52	416	12.50%	52.63	-107.91	45.38	1.06	1.37
Richard Hannon	51	372	13.71%	54.43	-1.61	39.85	1.23	1.36
Archie Watson	50	350	14.29%	56.19	-107.40	39.15	1.27	1.56
Richard Fahey	48	473	10.15%	52.82	-101.58	38.36	0.94	1.07

YARMOUTH

Trainer	Wins	Runs	Strike Rate	% Rivals Beaten	P/L	Run To Form %	Impact Value	Market Value
William Haggas	31	142	21.83%	62.55	-28.57	49.23	1.68	2.00
John Gosden	28	75	37.33%	78.57	12.53	66.90	2.95	2.49
Chris Wall	25	130	19.23%	54.86	-16.68	43.22	1.61	1.45
Michael Bell	24	126	19.05%	53.97	-10.70	48.76	1.53	1.22
John & Thady Gosden	20	69	28.99%	72.35	12.77	69.51	2.27	2.08
Roger Varian	20	115	17.39%	65.37	-32.98	53.55	1.46	1.86
Stuart Williams	18	181	9.94%	49.96	-20.50	34.01	0.76	1.09
Mark Johnston	18	122	14.75%	46.94	-37.35	42.62	0.97	1.24
David Simcock	17	113	15.04%	49.55	-29.38	42.57	1.04	1.26
Michael Appleby	15	187	8.02%	40.95	-69.68	22.93	0.67	0.89

YORK

Trainer	Wins	Runs	Strike Rate	% Rivals Beaten	P/L	Run To Form %	Impact Value	Market Value
Richard Fahey	37	498	7.43%	50.60	-153.25	29.54	0.85	1.12
William Haggas	32	193	16.58%	58.19	-38.73	47.19	1.72	2.15
Tim Easterby	31	488	6.35%	48.36	-26.38	24.71	0.82	1.06
David O'Meara	24	375	6.40%	50.32	-80.83	27.45	0.79	1.20
Mark Johnston	24	191	12.57%	48.80	5.35	32.85	1.25	1.24
Michael Dods	23	174	13.22%	58.56	9.92	33.53	1.67	1.48
John Gosden	21	70	30.00%	60.57	7.39	59.49	2.42	2.19
Kevin Ryan	19	293	6.48%	47.85	-128.38	26.62	0.74	1.15
Andrew Balding	18	147	12.24%	55.03	16.65	45.58	1.19	1.26
K. R. Burke	17	146	11.64%	55.34	-6.34	40.22	1.29	1.22

INDEX

Index To Photographs